a study guide for

From
Slavery
to
Freedom

fifth edition

a study guide for

From
Slavery
to
Freedom

fifth edition

Edward F. Sweat
Fuller E. Callaway Professor Emeritus of History
Clark College, Atlanta

Alfred A. Knopf   New York

THIS IS A BORZOI BOOK
PUBLISHED BY ALFRED A. KNOPF, INC.

First Edition

987654321

Copyright © 1980 by Alfred A. Knopf, Inc.

ISBN: 0-394-32474-9

Manufactured in the United States of America

ACKNOWLEDGMENT

P ORTIONS OF THIS publication originally appeared in a USAFI study guide, *History of the American Negro,* by Edward F. Sweat, Copyright 1970 by the Regents of the University of Wisconsin, and are reprinted by special permission.

CONTENTS

chapter **I**
Land of Their Fathers   1

chapter **II**
The African Way of Life   7

chapter **III**
The Slave Trade   13

chapter **IV**
Seasoning in the Islands   19

chapter **V**
Colonial Slavery   24

chapter **VI**
Latin America's Bondmen   30

chapter **VII**
That All Men May Be Free   35

chapter **VIII**
The Turn of the Century   41

chapter **IX**
The Westward March   46

chapter **X**
That Peculiar Institution   52

viii

chapter **XI**
Quasi-Free Negroes   58

chapter **XII**
Slavery and Intersectional Strife   64

chapter **XIII**
The Civil War   70

chapter **XIV**
The Effort to Attain the Peace   76

chapter **XV**
Losing the Peace   83

chapter **XVI**
Philanthropy and Self-Help   88

chapter **XVII**
Enlarged Dimensions of Racial Conflict   94

chapter **XVIII**
In Pursuit of Democracy   101

chapter **XIX**
Democracy Escapes   106

chapter **XX**
The Harlem Renaissance   111

chapter **XXI**
The New Deal   116

chapter **XXII**
Two Worlds of Race   121

chapter **XXIII**
Fighting for the Four Freedoms   126

chapter **XXIV**
The Postwar Years   131

chapter **XXV**
The Black Revolution   135

Key to Self-Test   141

INTRODUCTION

T HIS STUDENT STUDY Guide is designed to help you study and understand the material in the textbook *From Slavery to Freedom: A History of Negro Americans,* fifth edition, by John Hope Franklin.

Like *From Slavery to Freedom,* the Guide is divided into twenty-five chapters. To use the Study Guide to its fullest advantage, you should become familiar with its general pattern. As you examine the Guide, you will see that each chapter follows the same general plan: a chronology, an introductory statement, study notes, a self-test, which includes essay questions, an identify and/or define section, and, for some chapters, map study exercises.

Chronology. At the beginning of each chapter significant dates of events that are discussed in the text will be found. They will help you focus on the sequence of major events covered in that chapter.

Introductory Statement. An introduction at the beginning of each chapter gives the general nature and importance of the contents of the chapter and at times supplements chapter material. It may also direct your attention to points you should watch for in the material you are about to study.

Study Notes. The study notes direct your attention to specific pages in the text, amplifying or emphasizing points that deserve special emphasis. You may use the study notes when you do your reading assignment or, preferably, when you do a second, more rapid reading of the textbook. You should find the study notes helpful when reviewing for examinations.

Self-Test. This part contains exercises that help you test yourself on your knowledge of material covered in each chapter. Included are multiple choice, filling in blanks, and true-or-false items. They should tell you whether or not you have understood what you have read and how well you have retained subject matter material. The answers to these are given in the Key to Self-Test at the back of the Guide. You should try to answer as many as possible without referring either to the text or to the answers. Check your answers when you have completed all items. Included in this section are essay questions. These will require thought, organization, and the ability to communicate clearly, as well as basic knowledge of facts. Evaluate your answers here by referring afterward to the text or in some instances to supplementary sources.

Identify and/or Define. This section calls your attention to words, terms, and individuals covered in the chapter. Do not hesitate to use a standard dictionary if it becomes necessary.

Map Study. In some cases map exercises are relevant. They are designed to help you understand the geographical aspects of the textbook material. If necessary, supplement the maps found in the Guide with an historical atlas.

The serious use of this Guide can prove rewarding in terms of comprehension and of time saved that would otherwise be spent in aimless and undisciplined rereading of textbook material. The thoughtful and honest use of the Guide can help in a fuller, more complete understanding of the text.

chapter I

LAND OF THEIR FATHERS

Chronology

1062–1076	Reign of Tenkamenin in Ghana
1324	Pilgrimage of Mansa-Musa to Mecca
1469–1492	Reign of Sonni Ali in Songhay
1493–1529	Reign of Askia Mohammed in Songhay
1497	Pilgrimage of Askia Mohammed to Mecca

INTRODUCTORY STATEMENT

ONE OF THE more enduring myths about Africa is that of a dark continent, lacking in most of the paraphernalia of civilization. This myth was based largely on limited European contact with the people of Africa and a consequent lack of knowledge of Africa's past. Scholars and well-informed people now agree that from at least the fourth century A.D. centralized states had emerged in West Africa; that is, in the area running from the Atlantic to near the Nile, and from the Sahara in the north to the Gulf of Guinea in the South. Although some states declined and even disappeared, others arose to take their place and add to their number. On the eastern coast, the influence of Islam came to dominate most of the political entities to be found in that part of Africa.

With the passing of time, the locus of power in West Africa shifted from the savannah region to the coastal lands of the forest belt along the Gulf of Guinea. Among the better known of the organized political and economic units of this region, to Europeans, were Benin, Oyo, and Dahomey, primarily because of the slave trade.

STUDY NOTES

Page 3, *Early West African states.* Well-developed political states had arisen and declined before any lasting contact was established between this region and the Muslim Near East. The best known and most powerful of these early kingdoms were Ghana, Mali, and Songhay.

1

Pages 4–5, *Ghana*. The first recorded West African state was Ghana. Located roughly north of the Senegal and Niger rivers, its rise and growth were based primarily on commercial pursuits rather than on military conquest. Its black rulers were dispensers of both justice and rewards and were the heads of the indigenous religion. An eleventh-century king subsequently became a convert to Islam, and the Muslim influence became apparent. Despite economic benefits derived from Arab infiltration, religious strife, which developed between those who refused to accept Islam and those who became Muslims, undermined the kingdom. This strife, along with a period of stifling economic decline at the end of the eleventh century, so weakened the state that it became impossible to prevent conquest by twelfth- and thirteenth-century invaders.

Pages 4 and later, *Royal converts to Islam*. Note that black rulers who became Muslims took this step partly because they felt it was to their economic and political advantage. Such a move, however, produced tensions between African people who made the transition and those who retained their indigenous beliefs. This largely accounts for the religious strife that had the effect of upsetting internal harmony at various times and in various regions of West Africa.

Pages 5–7, *Mali*. A strongly organized kingdom about 1235 A.D., Mali supplanted and exceeded Ghana as a vibrant state. Although consolidated and strengthened by Sundiata Keita in the thirteenth century, the kingdom reached its greatest height in the fourteenth century under the leadership of Mansa-Musa. Converted to Islam, members of the Keita dynasty demonstrated their piety and devotion by making the traditional pilgrimage to Mecca. The account of the historic journey of Mansa-Musa reveals a good deal about the level of attainment of Mali in this period. This event was also a display of wealth and power. The very size of the entourage, the amount of gold used to finance this remarkable pilgrimage, and the generous dispensing of gifts on the way to Mecca were all calculated to reflect a stable kingdom ruled by a powerful and affluent, but benevolent, ruler. Note that this demonstration of political, economic, and social stability was possible at a time when European states had not yet achieved national unity. In the fifteenth century, attacks from combined outside forces contributed to the decline and disintegration of the kingdom and a consequent reduction of its power and influence.

Pages 7–8, *Songhay*. As Mali's power and influence declined, that of Songhay grew. Successor state to Mali, it became West Africa's most powerful empire. Earlier it had come under the influence of Mali after the capture of Gao by soldiers of Mansa-Musa. After becoming vassals of this strong ruler and his successors, the Songhay waited for an opportunity to assert their sovereignty. A Songhay prince, held as a hostage for a time by Mansa-Musa, escaped and returned to his people where he founded the new and virile dynasty of the Sonnis.

Page 9, *The Sonni dynasty*. The last king of this line, Sonni Ali, who came to the throne in 1464, succeeded in making Songhay the strongest kingdom in West Africa. At the time of his death, in 1492, Songhay was recognized as the major power in the region.

Page 9, *The reign of Askia Mohammed*. Partly because of internal religious conflicts, the dynasty of the Sonnis was overthrown in the next year by a devout Muslim general, Askia Mohammed, a former subordinate of Sonni Ali. This brilliant leader strengthened and expanded the empire through military conquest.

Pages 9–10, *Intellectual activity.* As an orthodox Muslim, Askia Mohammed made the pilgrimage to Mecca in 1497, using the occasion as a means of adding to the international stature of his realm. Scholars who accompanied him as part of his retinue made helpful contacts with their peers in the East. Reforms suggested on the pilgrimage were set in motion upon Askia Mohammed's return to Songhay. As a result, political and economic activities were made more efficient. Significant advances were made in the area of education; schools were established and encouraged in various parts of the empire. Gao, Walata, Timbukta, and Jenne were intellectual centers, and attracted scholars from West Africa, Asia, and Europe.

Weaker than Askia Mohammed, his successors were unable to prevent either the internal decline that beset the kingdom, or invasions by Moors who eventually conquered the Songhay kingdom.

Pages 11–13, *Other states.* Other well-organized and economically sound states emerged and prospered in West Africa. The disintegration of Songhay resulted in a more immediate shift in power and economic influence to such states as Hausa and Bornu. Gradually, the locus of power in West Africa shifted from the savannah states of the Sudan to states located in the forest belt.

Page 13, *Europeans come to trade.* Situated along the Gulf of Guinea, these centers attracted the interest of the Portuguese in the fifteenth century as they explored the West African coast. Two of the more substantial were the empires of Benin and Kongo, with whom the Portuguese rapidly developed profitable trade relations. The discovery of America, with a subsequent search for labor with which to develop the lands of the New World, led to a trade in human beings which unfortunately became the area's most coveted form of commerce. Other states that were negatively affected by this traffic were Oyo and Dahomey.

Page 13, *Summary.* The conquest of Africa by newly industrialized nations of Europe reached its height in the nineteenth century and resulted in a division of much of Africa. Many Europeans could comfort themselves with the specious reasoning that Africa was a dark continent, inhabited by a backward people who needed the oversight of more civilized nations.

This chapter contains a description of only some of the political units of West Africa. That other regions of this vast continent have not been examined is not meant to minimize the importance of states that developed and prospered in these areas.

SELF-TEST

Do you understand what you have read in this chapter? Can you remember the most important concepts, ideas, and events? Without referring to the text, answer as many of the following questions as you can. When you have completed all items in the Self-Test section, check your answers with the Key to Self-Test at the back of the Guide.

Multiple Choice

1. The first West African state of which there is any record is:
   a. Mali.
   b. Ghana.
   c. Empire of the Congo.
   d. Dahomey.

2. A comparison of Europe and West Africa in the middle of the fourteenth century would show that:
   a. no state had emerged in West Africa.
   b. states had been established in West Africa, but all had been founded and ruled by whites.
   c. no national state had arisen in either place.
   d. European states had not yet achieved national unity, but well-developed states ruled by blacks had appeared in West Africa.

3. Which of the following represents the correct chronological order?
   a. Ghana, Mali, Songhay.
   b. Ghana, Songhay, Mali.
   c. Songhay, Mali, Ghana.
   d. Mali, Songhay, Ghana.

4. All of the following help to explain the decline and eventual disintegration of Songhay *except:*
   a. the outbreak of civil and religious wars.
   b. unsuccessful military expeditions.
   c. failure to establish centers of formal educational activity.
   d. invasions by Moors armed with guns.

5. Which of the following is the *least* important reason why certain black African rulers became Muslims?
   a. the prospect of expanded trade opportunities.
   b. the pressure of public opinion.
   c. religious conviction.
   d. the enhancement of political power.

Fill in the Blanks

1. _MECCA_ The name of the holy city of Islam to which certain West African Muslim kings made religious pilgrimages.

2. _MALI_ The Negro kingdom that supplanted and exceeded the heights attained by Ghana.

3. _Sundiata Keita_ He is credited with consolidating and strengthening the kingdom of Mali.

4. _ASKia Mohammed_ Referred to as Songhay's most brilliant ruler.

5. _Slave trade_ This traffic in humans became the most dominant form of commerce engaged in by African states along the Gulf of Guinea.

True or False

_F_ 1. Arabs were responsible for introducing civilization to West Africa.

_F_ 2. The boundaries of early Ghana were the same as are those of its modern namesake.

_T_ 3. The nucleus of Mali's political organization dates back to the beginning of the seventh century.

_T_ 4. Mansa-Musa's pilgrimage to Mecca was as much a display of wealth and power as it was a holy journey.

_T_ 5. The strength of the Mossi states lay in their efficient political and military system.

Essay Questions

The following will require the ability to assimilate, organize, and communicate clearly the basic facts of this chapter.

1. Develop the proposition that the history of political states in West Africa contradicts the concept of Africa as the "dark continent."
2. Trace briefly the rise and decline of any one of the major states examined in this chapter.
3. What similarities can you see among the states of Ghana, Mali, and Songhay? In what ways did they differ?
4. Compare and contrast the pilgrimages to Mecca of Mansa-Musa and Askia Mohammed.
5. What effects did the coming of the Portuguese have on the political stability and economy of the forest belt states?

Identify and/or Define

Throughout the Guide, the following section will contain terms, words, and the names of people and places you are to identify. Use a dictionary wherever it becomes necessary.

myth	savannah	Mecca
state	entourage	Kaaba
indigenous	delta	Muslim
dynasty	*fari* Governors	Islam
sudan	*noi* chiefs	

6

Map Study

On this outline map, locate as exactly as possible the states of Ghana, Mali, and Songhay. Do the same for such lesser entities as Bornu, Kanen, the Mossi states, Oyo, and Dahomey.

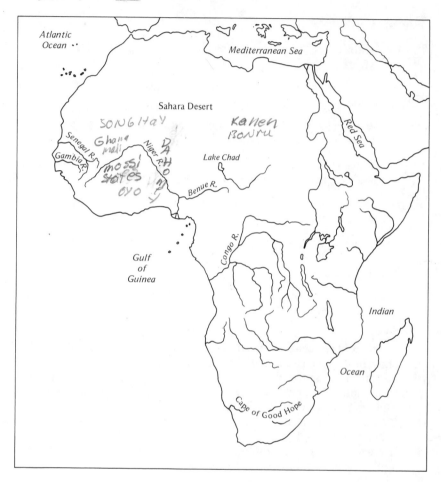

Map 1. Africa, 700–1500 A.D.

chapter II

THE AFRICAN
WAY OF LIFE

Chronology

Ca. 500 B.C.–Ca. 200 A.D.	The Nok Culture
Ca. 1550 A.D.–Ca. 1690 A.D.	Benin Sculpture

INTRODUCTORY STATEMENT

A S IN OTHER parts of the world, the way of life in Africa until about the end of the sixteenth century varied in degrees of civilization from primitive to highly advanced. Within the continent itself was a variety of geographical and physical features, differences among the people, a diversity of cultures, and a multiplicity of spoken languages. Even when attention is focused on West Africa, whence came most of those who were transported to America, these factors operate to discourage unlimited generalizations about the patterns of behavior of the people. Most authorities agree that the early West African states were based on agriculture, tending of livestock, ironworking, and commercial activities. Basic to their political development were hierarchic political organizations with ruling groups and families.

In all the paraphernalia of social organization—government, law, religion, rules of conduct, economic activity, esthetic expression—African society was as complex as ours.

STUDY NOTES

Pages 15–16, *Political institutions.* Throughout Africa there were forms of political organization, ranging from the simple to the sophisticated. In some sections the family state, whose leader was the head of the family, prevailed. If the constituents of a number of such states claimed a common ancestry, a more potent entity known as the clan state might be formed. In turn, a larger and even more potent village state or tribe seat might be created when groups of such clan states agreed to cooperate as a political unit.

The merger of village states, either voluntarily or by force, resulted in the formation of small kingdoms, described as the most popular form of government in Africa. From such kingdoms grew federations and empires such as Mali and Songhay.

These states shared the same essential characteristics. There was a royal family from which came the ruler, who was chosen by an electing family and vested in office by persons designated by the enthroning family.

Page 16, *Powers of rulers not absolute.* That the electing family exercised substantial authority is seen in its ability to make a choice as to which male member of the royal family would become the ruler. Ministers and other advisors, functioning as a kind of parliament, assisted the kings in administering the affairs of the realm. By custom, many kings were denied the authority to settle questions involving the land of their kingdoms, unless they were descendants of the land's first occupants. Along with this limit on the power of African kings was the degree of autonomy and authority exercised by local royal personages within the latters' localities.

Pages 17–18, *Economic life.* Although essentially agricultural, the peoples of Africa did not devote their time and energies solely to this economic pursuit. Note that land was held individually or collectively and was highly valued, even though final ownership was vested in those who were the first occupants of the soil. Other pursuits involved the raising and tending of domesticated animals and fowl.

Artisanry, as practiced by early Africans, reveals a remarkable degree of skill in the art of basket-making, weaving, the creation of woodwork, and metallurgy.

Authorities disagree as to whether or not the use and making of iron were first discovered by Africans or Hittites. Its use was developed very early in Africa, with some being used locally and some exported. African artisans and smiths worked in silver, gold, copper, and bronze, producing implements and ornamental objects of both utility and esthetic worth.

Pages 18–19, *Commercial and cultural contacts.* That early Africans were not simply provincials in their outlook or actions is reflected in the keen attention devoted to commerce. Whether trading with other African groups or with other states, a lively and profitable exchange of goods developed. Among the more prized items were gold, silver, and with the passing of time, humans. These commercial contacts, based on the exchange of goods, also facilitated the exchange of culture traits between Africa and other parts of the world.

Pages 19–20, *Social organization.* The family was the basis of social organization in early Africa. The eldest male was usually head of the family, but the practice of tracing or designating descent through the mother was widespread. Polygamy existed in virtually every region, but it was not universally practiced.

Pages 20–21, *Social mobility.* Although signs of social stratification appeared early, social mobility was possible. Families, rather than individuals, constituted the classes of the traditional social structure. Families were degraded or dignified on the basis of the types of work they did. Note that no matter what their level, all persons were regarded as individuals worthy of respect and accorded privileges earned by acknowledged skills.

Pages 21–22, *African slavery.* The practice of slavery was of early origin and widespread, and represented a significant feature of the social and economic life of Africa. Predominantly persons captured in war, they were by law chattel property, but in practice they were often accorded substantial privileges and virtual freedom. Children of slaves could not be sold, and were often manumitted.

Page 22, *Religion*. The majority of Africans practiced the indigenous religion, even after the introduction of Islam and Christianity. The religion of early Africans revolved around the belief that the spirits of their ancestors had unlimited power over their lives. The spirits of early ancestors, those who were first on the ground, were the most revered. The religion was animistic, as is seen by the belief that spirits or souls dwelt in such objects as the family land, and trees and rocks native to the community. The priests of the religion were, logically enough, the patriarchs of the families.

Page 23, *Magic*. Just as has been true of others, Africans were affected by, and concerned with the supernatural forces over which they had no control. This largely accounts for the widespread belief in magic, whose practices were designed to help explain the forces and workings of the supernatural.

Pages 23-24, *Islam and Christianity*. The introduction of Islam and Christianity did not result in a mass conversion of black Africans to these faiths. Some rulers became Muslims for what they perceived to be practical reasons, but frequently subjects continued to practice the indigenous religion. Many Africans found it difficult to reconcile the preachings of Christianity with the practices and involvement of Christians in the slave trade.

Pages 24-25, *The arts*. Africans expressed themselves in sculpture, music, and dance. In such media as sculpture their work reveals a capacity for esthetic expression worthy of critical admiration and acclaim. Among the earliest extant examples of African sculpture are the terra cotta figures of the Nok culture, found in present-day Nigeria. These figures are an exciting example of skill in the fashioning of beautiful objects of art.

Page 25, *Music*. Music was an important medium of esthetic expression, with the most frequently utilized musical form being songs, with or without instrumental accompaniment. They ranged in type from lullabies and dance songs to work songs and sacred melodies. Traditionally associated with African music and dance is the drum, but other widely used musical instruments were the xylophone, guitar, zither, harp, and flute. The art of dancing was engaged in by Africans as a form of recreation and expression of community relationship, as well as for religious or ritualistic functions.

Pages 25-26, *African languages*. The many spoken languages in Africa have constituted a barrier to the development of written literary forms. Among those that have been classified are the Sudanic and Bantu groups. There are many others, including tribal dialects and languages having no apparent relationship to the principal groups. This heterogeneity in spoken language made the evolution of adequate means of extensive communication extremely difficult. Since few of the languages were reduced to writing, the literature was predominantly oral. This oral literature was varied in its subject matter, and presented to succeeding generations by individuals called griots, whose speciality was collecting and transmitting the oral history of their locality or kinship group. Use of Arabic by educated

Muslim Negroes made possible its use in developing a written literature among the Africans.

Pages 26–28, *The African way of life.* Europeans who began to make incursions into Africa in the fifteenth and sixteenth centuries came in contact with a way of life that in its essentials was as complex as theirs. Political entities were organized, whether basic or complex in form, and in their operation reflected a satisfactory balance between rulers and subjects. This general stability within states permitted, and even encouraged, a healthy economic development. Social institutions reflected to a marked degree the cohesive influence of the family unit, whether it was the immediate family, the clan, or the tribe. Religious practices can be understood largely in terms of the depth of loyalty and attachment of individuals to their families.

Preoccupation with the question of survival did not prevent attention from being paid to the esthetic aspects of life. Lives were enriched, whether through painting, sculpture, carving, or music and the dance. Their oral literature, handed down from one generation to another, served as a reminder of the past, a source of amusement, and a guide for social and political conduct. Their written literature, largely in Arabic, does not suffer by comparison with that of their contemporaries.

Page 28, *Transplantation of African culture.* There is still disagreement among students of Africa and America as to the extent to which this African culture was transplanted to the New World. Some contended that, since they were coming from the "dark continent," there was nothing for Africans who came as slaves to bring with them. Others could detect nothing in contemporary Negro life that could be traced to the African background. By way of contrast, some scholars have insisted that the African cultural heritage can be seen in many aspects of contemporary American life.

Pages 28–29, *The process of acculturation.* What can be said with certainty is that at least two acculturative processes went on simultaneously in the New World. There was an interaction of African cultures resulting from the living together of Africans who had come from different backgrounds and experiences. The new cultural patterns that resulted from this interaction were still rooted deeply in the African experience. At the same time, there was the interaction of African and Western cultures, which resulted in changes in the culture patterns of both groups. Wherever Africans were settled in the New World, some survival of the culture of Africa can be observed. These survivals bear testimony to the strength and tenacity of these traits of the African background, as well as to the resiliency inherent in African institutions.

SELF-TEST

Multiple Choice

1. In early African society, the eldest male was:
   a. usually head of the family.
   b. always head of the family.
   c. never head of the family.
   d. only rarely the head of the family.

2. Slavery as a feature of African life was:
   a. introduced to the continent by Europeans.
   b. an outgrowth of the need for a cheap labor supply.
   c. the result of a conscious effort to develop a caste society.
   d. widespread and of early origin.

3. The practice of polygamy was:
   a. forbidden in early Africa.
   b. denied to converts to Islam.
   c. permitted in virtually every region.
   d. encouraged by Christian missionaries.

4. The monarchs of West African political units were:
   a. rarely absolute rulers.
   b. elected on the basis of universal manhood suffrage.
   c. seldom, if ever, limited in their power.
   d. always the eldest son of the royal family.

5. Because of the family character of African religions:
   a. each family member was revered as a priest.
   b. belief in magic was rare and confined to one area.
   c. the priests of the religion were the patriarchs of the families.

Fill in the Blanks

1. _Small Kingdoms_ Referred to as the most popular form of government in early Africa.

2. _Electing family_ Charged with the responsibility of choosing the ruler of the state from among the male members of the royal family.

3. _Ancestor worship_ The most accurate description of the religion of early Africa.

4. _Family_ This unit was the basis of social organization in early Africa.

5. _Song_ With or without instrumental accompaniment, the most frequently used art form in Africa.

True or False

_F_ 1. Scholars agree that no part of the African heritage was transplanted or preserved by Africans in the New World.

_F_ 2. Africans were neither primarily nomadic nor simply agricultural.

_T_ 3. Kings were always members of the family of the first person occupying the ground in his state.

_T_ 4. The use of iron was developed very early in the economy of Africa.

_T_ 5. The need for a cheap domestic labor force accounts for the practice of slavery in Africa.

Essay Questions

1. Support the assertion that early African society in its government, codes of conduct, and social organization generally was as complex as ours.
2. Describe the various forms of political organization developed by the people of Africa. What essential characteristics were shared by the more complex forms?
3. What is meant by the statement that "it would be fallacious to assume that Africans were either primarily nomadic or simply agricultural"? Explain, illustrating your answer with examples.
4. Discuss the role of the family as the basis of, and as a cohesive influence in, the social organization of early Africa.
5. What were the basic characteristics of the indigenous religion of early Africa? How do you account for the widespread use of magic? How do you explain the limited success of Islam and Christianity in West Africa?

Identify and/or Define

clan	magic	terra cotta
patrilineal	griot	family state
matrilineal	culture	clan state
social stratification	culture trait	village state
animism	acculturation	tribe seat
artisanry		

chapter III

THE SLAVE TRADE

Chronology

1501	Spanish ban lifted on blacks going into its lands in the New World
1513–1528	Blacks accompanied such Spanish explorers as Balboa, Cortes, Pizarro, and Coronado
1528	Black explorer Estevanico opened up New Mexico and Arizona for Spaniards
Ca. 1790	Jean Baptiste Point du Sable erected first building on site of present Chicago
1517	Slave trade to New World *formally* began with Spanish official decision to supplement indigenous Indian work force with African slaves
1713	England granted *asiento* for thirty years

INTRODUCTORY STATEMENT

THE PORTUGUESE, who inaugurated the modern institution of slavery and the slave trade, did not introduce a new practice among the peoples of the world. The practice of enslaving human beings had appeared long before the fifteenth century in Africa and elsewhere. Slavery in Greece, Rome, Europe, and the Muslim world was different in many respects from the patterns that evolved in the New World. The slave's social status, duties and obligations, his mobility, and his economic standing varied at different times and in different places. To be a West African slave in the fifteenth century generally meant fewer disabilities and a far easier social role than to be a slave in the New World in the sixteenth and seventeenth centuries.

With limited potential for growth in Europe, the institution of slavery was given new life in the New World by the perceived need for a large labor force with which to exploit the hemisphere's natural resources. Securing slaves on the African west coast with the active cooperation of local potentates, and transporting them across the Atlantic to the Americas became a huge and lucrative business. This unsavory enterprise added to the coffers of individuals, of trading companies, and even of nations.

The estimate as to the exact number of persons involved in this black diaspora vary. Continuing for several hundred years, there is little question

14

that millions of slaves were imported into the New World, while large numbers died resisting capture or while en route during the middle passage. There is no way to quantify the effect of this expatriation on African life itself. The removal of the flower of African manhood was catastrophic, and had far-reaching negative effects on that part of Africa where civilization had reached an extremely high level. Never fully recovering from the trade itself, or from the internal dissension fostered by European traders, Africa fell prey to European colonizers in the nineteenth century.

STUDY NOTES

Page 30, *Early slavery.* Slavery was widespread during the earliest history of Africa, but at least in parts of the continent, there was no racial basis of slavery. The Muslim practice of seizing women for their harems and men for military and menial service gave an impetus to the development of the institution. Both by purchase and conquest, the Muslims recruited African slaves to be exported to Islamic lands. Thus, long before the extensive development of the slave trade in the hands of Europeans, many of the basic practices of the international trade had already been established.

Pages 31–32, *The modern institution of slavery and the slave trade.* The modern institution of slavery and the slave trade were created by forces set in motion by the Renaissance and the Commercial Revolution. It is pointed out here that the spirit of the Renaissance, with its sanction of ruthless freedom, along with the practice of the Commercial Revolution, with its new techniques of exploitation, conspired to bring forth new approaches to the acquisition of wealth and power. Among these was the establishment of the institution of modern slavery and the concomitant practice of importing and exporting slaves. Such new and powerful national states as Spain, Portugal, France, Holland, and Britain were the political instrumentalities through which these modern forces were channeled.

Page 33, *Slavery in Europe.* By the end of the fourteenth century, Europeans began to bring slaves into Europe. Aside from profits realized by traders, Europeans could justify this practice on the grounds that bringing Africans to Europe would give these heathen people the opportunity to become Christians. Primarily because of the nature of Europe's economic institutions, there was never any profitable future for African slavery on the European continent. It was in the New World, with its vast natural resources and undeveloped regions, that slavery and the slave trade eventually became profitable.

Pages 33–34, *Negroes come to the New World.* Black people accompanied the first Europeans who explored and opened the Western hemisphere. Serving in various capacities, they traveled with Spanish conquistadores, Portuguese explorers, and the French expeditions. Note that Negroes did not accompany the English on their explorations in the New World.

Pages 34–35, *Problem of inadequate labor supply.* The process of exploiting the New World's natural resources required the labor of many hands. Europeans experimented first with local peoples, ruthlessly exploiting them until some were almost exterminated. Susceptibility of native peoples to the diseases of Europeans, along with a lack of experience in working in the disciplined regime of the plantation system established by Europeans, all but eliminated them as satisfactory workers. This led to the search for other sources of labor.

Page 35, *White indentured servants.* The continued need for workers in large quantities helps to account for the introduction of the system of indentured servitude. Indentured servants were poor whites who, in return for their transportation to America, agreed to work for a stated period of years. When those who had voluntarily indentured themselves proved to be insufficient, the English resorted to such practices as raiding the prisons of England, and even kidnaping children, women, and drunken men in order to augment the labor supply. These white servants proved to be unsatisfactory for several reasons. Strictly controlled by their masters, servants received no compensation but their keep during their term of service. This was a constant source of irritation to servants, many of whom ran away or sued masters and ship captains for illegal detention. This was compounded by other related problems, but the most evident was that white indentured servitude did not solve the problem of an insufficient supply of workers.

Pages 35–36, *African slavery as a solution.* Englishmen gradually came to feel that the best possible labor force for their needs was the black African slave. Their color, pagan background, the fact that they could be purchased outright, and with the apparently inexhaustible supply, all contributed to persuade Englishmen that black slavery was the key to the solution of their labor problem. Not only did it answer the need for labor in America, but at the same time it erected for Europe an important economic institution, the slave trade.

Pages 36–37, *The big business of trading in human beings.* As the West Indian plantations grew in size and importance, the slave trade became a huge, profitable undertaking, employing thousands of persons and involving a capital outlay of millions of dollars. Portugal was the first European country to engage in the slave trade, but that did not give it a monopoly on the trade. Spain's exclusion from Africa by the papal arbitration of 1493 forced that nation to grant the privilege of transporting slaves to her colonies to other nations. This right or contract to supply Spanish colonies was the prized *asiento.*

Page 37, *The Dutch and the slave trade.* Breaking the Portuguese hold in West Africa, the Dutch gained a foothold on the coast. By the middle of the seventeenth century the Dutch were supplying slaves to the settlers of other European nations in the New World.

Pages 37–38, *England and the slave trade.* The continued demand for slaves led the companies of such other nations as France and England to challenge the Dutch as carriers and sellers of African slaves. The decisive defeats of the Dutch by the British and the French in the late seventeenth century had the effect of enhancing England's prestige in Africa. England's securing of the *asiento* in 1713, which gave to that country the exclusive right to supply Spanish colonies with slaves for thirty years, meant that by the eighteenth century Britain had emerged with a lion's share of the business of trading in humans.

Pages 39–40, *The machinery of the slave trade.* By the eighteenth cen-

16

tury the techniques and procedures involved in the handling of the traffic in slaves had been pretty well standardized. Trading posts or factories, located on the coast and established by Europeans, were the bases of operation. Stationed at each post or slave factory were factors, that is, slave traders who were on good terms with local potentates. Representing the African chief in arrangements for securing slaves were agents, or caboceers. The business of trading in slaves was complicated and frequently long-drawn out. Prospective slaves offered stiff resistance to their capture, sale, and transportation to the New World. Wars between tribes broke out when the members of one sought to capture members of another to sell them into slavery.

Pages 41–42, *One-way passage.* The voyage from the coast of Africa to the Americas, popularly referred to as the "middle passage," is described as a "veritable nightmare." Overcrowded conditions were common. (Note illustration on page 43 of the text.) A high incidence of epidemics and such diseases as smallpox help to explain the high mortality rate among those aboard ship. Inhumane conditions generally led some who got the chance to do so, to jump overboard, while others were permanently disabled by disease or were maimed from struggling against their chains. Despite the great expenses attached to the trade and the extensive loss sustained in the mortality of slaves in transit, the slave trade was a lucrative business.

Pages 42–43, *Estimate of number transported.* Note the figures given in the text, particularly the estimates of Professor Philip D. Curtin, as to the number of slaves imported into the New World between 1451 and 1870. It is pointed out that it is more difficult to measure the effect of the trade on African life than it is to estimate the number of persons removed. That it was responsible for the forced removal of the flower of African manhood, thus depriving the continent of an invaluable resource, is without question. Aside from this, the encouragement that European traders gave Africans to fight among themselves, with guns, made it more difficult for them to recover from the body blow that the trade had dealt them.

SELF-TEST

Multiple Choice

1. Three of the following statements are false. Which one is *true*?
   a. Slavery was nonexistent in early Africa.
   b. Slavery in Africa carried with it the stigma of innate inferiority.
   c. Slaves in Africa were essentially chattel property controlled by an extremely harsh slave code.
   d. Slaves were not used in Africa primarily as producers of goods from which wealth was derived.

2. Important to the slave-trading business was:
   a. the active cooperation of certain African chiefs.
   b. the desire of large numbers of Africans to migrate to the West Indies.
   c. the friendly relationship between Christian missionaries and Muslims.
   d. the convenient overland route between West and North Africa.

3. The African slave trade:
   a. quickened the tempo of the entire African economy.
   b. fostered a greater degree of cooperation between African tribes.
   (c.) left the African continent in a serious state of recession and decline.
   d. paved the way for the coming of the Industrial Revolution to Africa.

4. The voyage of slaves from Africa to the Americas is referred to as the:
   a. Northwest Passage.
   (b.) middle passage.
   c. triangular trade route.
   d. *asiento*.

5. According to the estimate of Professor Philip D. Curtin, the total number of slaves imported to the New World between 1451 and 1870 was:
   a. 1,341,100.
   b. 6,051,700.
   (c.) 9,566,100.
   d. 1,898,400.

Fill in the Blanks

1. _Renaissance_ and _Commercial revolution_ Forces let loose by these movements created the modern institution of slavery and the slave trade.

2. _fourteenth century_ At the end of this century Europeans themselves began to bring slaves into Europe.

3. _Estevanico_ Black explorer who is credited with opening New Mexico and Arizona for the Spaniards.

4. _Indentured servants_ Europeans who, in exchange for their passage to America, voluntarily sold their labor for a specified period of years.

5. _Portugal_ The first European country to engage in the African slave trade.

True or False

_F_ 1. The institution of slavery was introduced into Africa by Muslims.

_T_ 2. Some indentured servants were transported to America against their will.

_F_ 3. Of all European nations, Portugal realized the greatest profits from the slave trade.

_T_ 4. Africans offered stiff resistance to their capture, sale, and transportation to the New World.

_F_ 5. The term *middle passage* refers to the transfer of slaves from the African shore to the ship.

Essay Questions

1. The slave trade was not a new practice introduced into Africa by Europeans. *Explain.* Account for the rise of the "modern" institution of slavery and the slave trade.
2. Show how the need for labor in the New World fostered the development of the big business of trading in human beings and in securing a position for slavery in the New World.
3. Describe the machinery and mechanics of the business of trading in slaves. What were some effects of this trade on African life?
4. Explain why indentured servitude failed to solve the problem of a shortage of labor in the New World.
5. Identify and give the significance of (a) the *asiento,* (b) the middle passage, (c) British Royal African Company.

Identify and/or Define

asiento
Papal Line of
  Demarcation (1493)
the Renaissance
the Commercial
  Revolution

indentured servitude
  (voluntary and
  involuntary)
conquistador

British Royal African
  Company
factor
caboceer
middle passage

chapter IV

SEASONING IN THE ISLANDS

Chronology

1493	Pope Alexander VI divided non-European world between Spain and Portugal
1494	In the Treaty of Tordesillas, Spain and Portugal finalized division made by Pope in 1493
1562–1568	English captain John Hawkins took slaves to Spanish islands illicitly where they were sold
1667	Slave code, "Act to regulate the Negroes on the British Plantations" passed by Parliament

INTRODUCTORY STATEMENT

T HE SLAVE TRADE became a tremendously important factor in European economic life primarily because of developments in the New World. Slaves were first transported to the islands of the Caribbean during the seventh century, where Europeans launched a serious effort to develop a profitable agricultural economy in the New World. Islanders experimented in producing a variety of crops, but it was the eminently successful cultivation of sugarcane that created an acute demand for labor. Increasingly planters came to feel that the most satisfactory answer to the labor shortage lay in the importation of slaves from Africa.

Upon arrival in the West Indies slaves were required to undergo a process of seasoning designed to accustom them to the ways of life in the plantation environment. In some places the novices were segregated and supervised by a special staff of functionaries who were experienced in the "breaking in" of new arrivals who might be recalcitrant.

Because slavery was important almost exclusively for economic reasons, there was little regard for the slave as a person. Slaves were thought of first and foremost as producers; thus evidence of humanitarianism among the planters, most of whom remained in Europe, is rare. The chief function of the overseer, who supervised plantation activities, was to produce wealth for the absentee landlord. This helps to account for the absence of social institutions that might have had an ameliorating effect on the everyday life of the black workers.

STUDY NOTES

Pages 45–46, *The Caribbean scene.* The slave trade might well have remained insignificant had it been confined to the importation of a few black workers into Europe. It became an important economic factor primarily because of agricultural developments in the New World particularly, at first, in the Caribbean. Partly because of the papal arrangement of 1493, Spain concentrated its attention on the development of its insular possessions. On these islands such staple crops as tobacco were produced with slave labor. Although firmly established in the New World by 1600, Spain lost all claim to exclusive control over the West Indies to other European powers in the seventeenth century. Taking the lead in breaking the Spanish monopoly in the Caribbean was the English sea captain John Hawkins.

Pages 46–48, *The plantation system.* Negroes were first used on the tobacco plantations of the islands, but, as noted earlier, it was the cultivation of sugarcane that led to a demand for laborers who were sufficient in number and "satisfactory" in conduct. This led planters to import more and more blacks from Africa as a solution to their problem. In the process, there developed a tendency to "overpopulate" the islands, a tendency that arose from at least two important factors. Consequently, many slaves brought into the islands were reexported. In addition, the mortality rate was so high that it exceeded the birth rate.

Page 48, *The nature of the institution.* Since slavery in the islands was essentially, almost exclusively, an economic institution, little attention was paid to the slave as a human being. This, coupled with the high degree of absentee landlordism, contributed to practices that were manifestly destructive of health and life among the slaves.

Pages 49–50, *The seasoning process.* Novices among the slave population were required to undergo a period of seasoning to prepare them for the rigors of plantation life. Note that the mortality rate during the seasoning period, which lasted from three to four years generally, was exceptionally high. Despite the inadequacy and the insufficiency of food, both male and female seasoned slaves were compelled to work long hours with only brief periods of rest provided.

Pages 50–51, *Caribbean black codes.* All of the West Indian colonies enacted, or had enacted for them, a body of regulatory laws under which slaves were governed. These laws varied from island to island, as did their application. Note, for example, the British "Act to regulate the Negroes in the British Plantations" of 1667, which referred to the blacks as "of wild, barbarous, and savage nature to be controlled only with strict severity." Although treatment under these codes varied, slaves enjoyed little protection against vicious and often inhuman practices.

Pages 51–52, *Slave resistance.* Despite cruel practices designed to keep slaves in a state of submission, there were numerous examples of slave resistance. These ranged from running away through conspiracies, uprisings, and revolts. Runaways in Jamaica and Haiti, called Maroons, so harassed the planters that in some instances the colonial governments officially had to recognize certain groups of them. Revolt, along with other manifestations of discontent, were common to all the West Indian colonies.

Pages 52–53, *Decline in the islands.* As the prosperity of the islands declined, slavery became less profitable. One significant manifestation of social and economic debility which set in during the early part of the eighteenth century was the increasing exportation of blacks from the West Indies to the mainland of North America.

SELF-TEST

Multiple Choice

1. The slave trade became a tremendously important factor in European economic life:
   a. primarily because of the need for unskilled labor in English factories.
   b. after the refusal of Europeans to work in service occupations.
   c. primarily because of developments in the New World.
   d. because of all of the above.

2. Three of the following are false. Which one is *true*?
   a. It was on the North American mainland that slavery began its really significant growth.
   b. Newly arrived slaves in the West Indies were forced to undergo a "seasoning" process.
   c. Africans were first brought to the Caribbean islands as indentured servants.
   d. The middle passage refers to the journey from the West Indies to the American mainland.

3. Plantation slaves in the West Indies were:
   a. most often supervised directly by their owners.
   b. engaged primarily in the cultivation of cotton.
   c. generally left in the hands of overseers whose chief concern was to produce wealth for their employers.
   d. seldom, if ever, discontented with their lot.

4. Which of the following helps to account for the increased exportation of slaves from the islands to the mainland in the eighteenth century?
   a. the preference of the mainland colonies for "seasoned" slaves.
   b. a world market glutted with sugar.
   c. soil exhaustion in the islands.
   d. all of the above.

5. The West Indian islands became of "immense importance to the grandeur and prosperity" of European nations primarily because of their value as:
   a. markets for European commodities.
   b. places to which surplus population could be settled.
   c. producers of revenue from sugar.
   d. sources of manufactured goods.

Fill in the Blanks

1. _Tobacco_ Negroes were first used on Caribbean plantations that grew this product.

2. _Spain_ European nation that took the lead in settling Caribbean islands.

3. _Seasoning_ Term applied to the practice of "breaking-in" newcomers in the islands' slave populations.

4. _black codes_ Repressive, regulatory body of laws under which slaves were governed.

5. _maroons_ Name given to runaway slaves in such islands as Jamaica and Haiti.

True or False

_F_ 1. The slave trade was never an important factor in European economic life.

_T_ 2. In the seventeenth century Spain lost all claim to exclusive control over islands of the Caribbean.

_F_ 3. Negroes were first used as workers on the sugarcane plantations of the West Indies.

_F_ 4. West Indian planters were noted for their humane treatment of slaves.

_T_ 5. On many islands of the Caribbean, blacks outnumbered whites.

Essay Questions

1. Account for the development of the slave trade as an important factor in European economic life.
2. Describe and give the significance of the seasoning, or breaking-in, process.
3. How do you explain the tendency of planters to overpopulate the islands with slaves? What connection can you see between this and absentee landlordism?
4. Argue for or against the proposition that the slave codes completely served the purpose for which they were intended.
5. What was the significance of a developing practice of exporting slaves from the islands to the mainland?

Identify and/or Define

the Caribbean	absentee landlordism	Maroons
seasoning	deleterious	sugarcane
slave code	mortality rate	

chapter V

COLONIAL SLAVERY

Chronology

1619	Twenty Africans landed at Jamestown, Virginia, beginning the forced importation of black people into the English North American colonies
1661	Statutory recognition of slavery in Virginia
1688	Germantown Quakers issue first formal protest against slavery
1712, 1741	Slave insurrections in New York
1739	Stono rebellion in South Carolina
1750	Prohibition against slavery in Georgia repealed

INTRODUCTORY STATEMENT

E NGLISH COLONISTS found on mainland America, as they had in the West Indies, a plentiful supply of land and, particularly in the South, geographic features that fostered the development of an agricultural economy. While land was plentiful, labor was scarce. Here, too, attempts to make use of Indians as workers proved to be unsuccessful. During much of the seventeenth century, white indentured servants imported from Europe largely made up the labor force. Preferred initially because of their cheapness, certain negative factors connected with their use made them unsatisfactory in the long run. Increased demands for labor prompted the colonists to look for the answer in the use of African slaves. These "perpetual servants" seemed not to present the problems inherent in the utilization of other types of servile labor.

In the summer of 1619, twenty Negroes were left at Jamestown in Virginia by a Dutch frigate. This marked the beginning of the forced importation of black people into the North American mainland, a movement that was not to end for more than 200 years. For the first forty years or so, these immigrants of African descent occupied a position of indentured servitude. Despite the fact that statutory recognition of slavery in Virginia did not come until 1661, by the end of the century slavery was firmly entrenched.

Among the workers of the middle colonies, which made up the region lying south and west of New England and stretching halfway down the Atlantic plain, were black men and women. These laborers, both slave and free, were employed in a variety of occupations which reflected the diversified nature of the region's economy. By and large, however, these colonies were more interested in slaves as commodities of commerce than as laborers. Although the treatment of blacks varied, in the areas of heavy Quaker settlement there was considerable respect for Negroes as human beings.

Even though the economy of New England did not lend itself to the widespread use of African slave labor, the institution became a fixture in that region during colonial times. After the region's merchants became deeply involved in the lucrative African slave trade, Puritans found their greatest justification for slavery. They argued that it could be justified on spiritual as well as on economic grounds, in much the same way as did their colonial neighbors in the southern colonies.

STUDY NOTES

Pages 54–55, *Black laborers: Virginia.* The earliest blacks in Virginia occupied a position similar to that of white servants in the colony. This position, however, did not last indefinitely. The failure of Indian servitude and the unsatisfactory nature of white indentured servitude created a vexing problem. The answer appeared to be in a fuller utilization of Negroes as "perpetual servants." Virginians came to recognize that blacks could not escape easily without being identified; that they could be disciplined or punished with impunity since they were not Christians; and that the supply seemed inexhaustible. The evolution from black servitude to slavery in the Virginia colony can be traced through developing practice and statute. By 1640 some Africans had become bondmen for life, with a clear distinction made between white indentured servants whose terms of indenture ended after a stated period of years, and Negroes who could be condemned to a period of "perpetual servitude." Actual statutory recognition of slavery in Virginia came in 1661. Other laws followed, culminating with one in 1667 which provided that "the conferring of baptisme" did not alter the condition of a person as to his bondage or freedom.

Pages 56 and later, *Slave code.* The growth of the slave population and the pervasive fear of slave insurrection led to the emergence of a body of laws that were designed to keep the Negroes under control. These laws appeared in all colonies and had certain features in common. They were negative in their nature, far-reaching in their effect, and they circumscribed the freedom of movement of slaves. In the South particularly they deprived the slaves of practically all civil, judicial, social, and political rights. These codes were enforced generally with severity, especially during periods of insurrection or when there was a rumor of a slave revolt.

Pages 56–57, *Maryland.* Slavery was not recognized by law in this colony until 1663, but by then the enslavement of blacks had been in practice for almost three decades. Note laws that had the effect of firmly establishing slavery on a statutory basis, as well as those dealing with the conduct and activities of slaves.

Pages 58–60, *The Carolinas.* The Carolina proprietors made provisions for slavery even before the region was settled. Note John Locke's *Fundamental Constitutions* and its reference to Negro slaves. Encouragement of the importation of Negroes into Carolina by the proprietors resulted in the presence of black people in the colony virtually from its beginning. By 1724 there were three times as many blacks as whites in Carolina, a disproportion that was a continuing cause of alarm among the whites. Revolts and rumors of plots to rebel led to harsh action and to the addition of more stringent provisions to the slave code. Some attempts were made to ameliorate conditions among the slaves by the Society for the Propagation of the Gospel in Foreign Parts.

In 1712 North Carolina was formally separated from South Carolina. The presence of Quakers in North Carolina, the relative smallness of the slave population, the early dispersion of the total population, and the impoverished state of many of the inhabitants all had a salutary effect on conditions among the black workers in this colony. These factors help to explain why there was no real slave insurrection in this area during the colonial period.

Page 60, *Georgia.* The last of the original thirteen English colonies to be founded, Georgia differed from the others in certain significant ways. Managed by a group of trustees, certain restrictions were placed on settlers. No free land titles were to be granted, alcoholic beverages were not permitted, and slavery was banned. At first denied the use of slaves, Georgians through continued agitation were able by 1750 to have the prohibition on slave ownership removed. Georgia was free from insurrection during its brief colonial period, but slaves resisted their enslavement by running away into Spanish Florida and by committing acts of sabotage.

Page 60, *Workers in the middle colonies.* In these colonies slaves were more important as commodities of commerce than as workers. Nevertheless, blacks were used fairly extensively on some farms.

Pages 61–62, *New York and New Jersey.* Slavery became entrenched early in New York as an important economic institution. Adoption of a stringent slave code failed to prevent dramatic slave rebellions in the colony in the years 1712 and 1741. After the English came to dominate New Jersey they encouraged slavery in every way.

Pages 62–63, *Pennsylvania.* Early in its history, strong objections to slavery were raised on moral and ethical grounds. Note the Germantown protest of 1688. The presence of Quakers in Penn's colony helps to explain the comparative mildness of the institution there. Aside from some moral opposition, white shopkeepers, artisans, and small farmers objected to slavery as a source of unfair competition.

Pages 62–63, *Failure of slavery.* As an economic institution, slavery had largely failed in the middle colonies before the end of the colonial period. Added to the fact that the region's economy did not lend itself to the extensive use of servile labor was some antipathy for the institution on moral grounds. These two factors help to explain why slavery was unsuccessful in the region.

Pages 63–64, *Colonial New England.* The arrival of blacks in New England in 1638 opened up new opportunities for the procurement of workers and for traffic in a commodity important to the commercial life of the region. In these colonies slavery was established by custom before being fixed by law.

Page 64, *New England characteristics.* The slaves of Puritan masters did not feel the stringent oppression that southern slaves experienced. Despite this relative mildness, freedom was preferred to bondage and many took positive steps to secure it. Throughout the colonial period, masters in New England held a firm hand on the institution of slavery and gave little attention to the small minority that argued for the freedom of slaves.

SELF-TEST

Multiple Choice

1. The twenty blacks who were brought to Jamestown in 1619:
   a. were immediately deported.
   b. were slaves under existing Virginia law.
   c. were "seasoned" and then sent to the West Indies.
   d. occupied a position similar to that of white indentured servants.

2. Three of the following concerning colonial slave codes are false. Which one is *true*?
   a. They provided the method by which manumission by owners was made easy.
   b. Civil and political rights of slaves were safeguarded.
   c. They were regulatory in nature and designed to suppress rebellion and control conduct.
   d. Under the codes, slaves had complete freedom of movement and assembly.

3. Which of these was *not* a restriction placed on the early settlers of Georgia?
   a. no freedom of worship.
   b. no free land titles.
   c. no slaves.
   d. no alcoholic beverages.

4. The middle colonies were interested in slaves primarily as:
   a. plantation laborers.
   b. commodities of commerce.
   c. replacements for white indentured servants.
   d. house servants.

5. Slave resistance in the middle colonies found its most dramatic expression in:
   a. Pennsylvania.
   b. New Jersey.
   c. Delaware.
   d. New York.

6. In 1688 a group of Quakers meeting at Germantown, Pennsylvania, drew up a celebrated protest against:
   a. the trend toward abolishing slavery.
   b. the teaching of blacks to read.
   c. the providing of religious instruction to slaves.
   d. slavery and the slave trade.

7. Shippers and merchants of New England benefited from:
   a. slave labor in their extensive manufacturing activities.
   b. the work of slaves in their rice fields.
   c. active participation in the slave trade.
   d. servile labor on their tobacco plantations.

8. During the colonial period slavery was a legal institution:
   a. only in the South.
   b. in all thirteen of the colonies.
   c. only in the middle colonies.
   d. in the southern and middle colonies, but not in New England.

Fill in the Blanks

1. _Virginia_ The landing of Negroes in this English colony marked the beginning of the forced importation of black people into the North American mainland.

2. _Georgia_ At the time of its founding, slavery was banned in this colony.

3. _Quakers_ The religious group largely responsible for the comparatively slow growth of slavery in Pennsylvania.

4. _New England_ This region's primary interest in slavery was in the slave trade.

5. _New York_ Middle colony that was the scene of two dramatic slave insurrections.

True or False

_F_ 1. The twenty Africans who were landed at Jamestown in 1619 were legally recognized as slaves.

_F_ 2. At the time of its founding, slavery was banned in the Carolina colony.

_T_ 3. Statutory recognition of slavery in Virginia did not come until the year 1661.

_T_ 4. During the colonial period slavery was a legal institution in all thirteen colonies.

_T_ 5. Despite the comparative mildness of slavery in New England, many slaves demonstrated dissatisfaction with their lot.

Essay Questions

1. Show the connection between the need for an adequate labor supply and the coming of slavery in Virginia.
2. In what respects was the Georgia colony different from the others at the time of its establishment? From what you know of the reasons for its founding, how do you account for these differences?
3. On what grounds can you explain the absence of full-scale slave insurrections in Pennsylvania?
4. Account for the failure of slavery as a viable economic institution in the middle colonies.
5. Trace the evolution from black servitude to slavery in the Virginia colony.

Identify and/or Define

Society for the Propagation of
  the Gospel in Foreign Parts
Quakers

The Germantown Protest
  of 1688
frigate

chapter VI

LATIN AMERICA'S BONDMEN

Chronology

1501 Spanish government authorizes the introduction of Africans into Spanish America
1538 First shipment of Africans reaches Brazil
1794 French National Convention ratifies proclamation of freedom for slaves in French colonies
1807 England outlaws the slave trade
1833 Compensated abolition of slavery in British possessions
1888 Final emancipation of slaves in Brazil

INTRODUCTORY STATEMENT

T HE ATTEMPT OF Spaniards in the New World to use the Indians as a forced labor supply ended in failure. To make up for the deficiency, the government authorized the importation of Africans into its colonies as early as 1501. By the year 1516 provisions had been made for the systematic transportation of slaves into Spanish colonies. Barred from the west coast of Africa, and viewing the slave trade as un-Christian and illegal, the practice of granting contracts or special permission known as the *asiento* was begun. The *asiento* conferred upon the recipient monopoly rights to supply the Spanish colonies with slaves. Under this arrangement, millions of Africans were imported to Spanish America.

These black workers were dispersed throughout Spanish America, in insular as well as continental possessions, from the Caribbean to the Pacific coast. A noticeable characteristic of the introduction of blacks into Latin America was the high degree of biological and cultural fusion that occurred.

The Portuguese, pioneers in the African slave trade, also furnished their New World empire with slave labor. The growth of the Negro population of Brazil was constant, so that by the end of the nineteenth century they represented a considerable proportion of the total population.

As was true of their brethren in other parts of the New World, Latin America's bondmen expressed dissatisfaction with their lot. Their resentment was reflected in uprisings of varying degrees of violence. These outbreaks led to the adoption of a body of laws and decrees that were designed to control and preserve order among slaves. One of the most dramatic and desperate bids for freedom in the New World occurred in Brazil in the seventeenth century. This was the establishment of the black state of Palmares in northeastern Brazil from 1630 to 1697.

Some scholars contend that slavery in colonial Latin America was not as harsh as its counterpart in English America. They point to the salutary influence of the Catholic church, the wide area over which a relatively small number of slaves was dispersed, and the greater respect accorded black people as human beings by both Spaniards and Portuguese who settled in Brazil.

The United States was neither the first nor the last country in the Western hemisphere to free its slaves. Haiti was the first of these nations to abolish slavery, with Brazil completing the emancipation process finally in 1888. Despite some opposition to the legal abolition of slavery throughout Latin America, the abolition process was generally free from the bitterness and hostility that it encountered in the United States.

STUDY NOTES

Pages 65–66, *Spanish slavery and the* asiento. As stated earlier, the Spanish attempt to utilize the forced labor of Indians was unsuccessful. In order to compensate for the continued need for laborers, the Spaniards turned to Africa as a source. The systematic importation of slaves to Spanish colonies was provided by the *asiento*. This was the exclusive privilege or contract granted by the Spanish king to others for supplying the colonies in America with slaves. This arrangement made it relatively easy for the crown to control the trade, as well as the numbers imported.

Pages 66–68, *Lebensraum*. Slaves were dispersed throughout Spanish America. They were transported to Mexico, Panama, Colombia, Peru, and Argentina, and from these points moved in all directions. In some areas they became mixed so extensively with whites and Indians that they were not recognizable as a distinct element in the population. This remarkable biological and cultural fusion that occurred throughout Spanish America shows the degree to which blacks were absorbed into the total population. It is also strongly suggestive of the apparent lack of color prejudice of the Spanish colonials.

Pages 68–70, *Adjustment in the New World*. Blacks in Spanish America were primarily agricultural workers. They were also used on large ranches, in the mines, and in a variety of occupations in urban areas. Slaves were both a source of profit and trouble. They frequently became restive and sought to gain their freedom. Acts of violence against persons and property culminated at times in full-scale insurrection. The body of laws and decrees, or slave code, that resulted had the essential characteristics of other slave codes. Although regulatory and negative in nature, the attempt was made to provide for the general welfare, religious instruction, and a moderate amount of free time for the slaves.

Page 70, *Nature of the institution*. Slavery in colonial Spanish America was perhaps not as harsh as the institution in English America. A number of influences mitigated the harshness of the institution. Note the involvement of the Catholic church in the slaves' lives. A second salutary influence was the wide area over which a relatively small number of slaves was dispersed; this provided more Lebensraum in which both master and slave could assert themselves. Finally, there was greater respect for Africans as human beings than there was in English America. It is pointed out that the willingness of Spaniards to intermarry with Negroes is ample proof of this.

Pages 71–72, *Slavery in Brazil.* Africans were introduced into Brazil as early as 1538. Note census figures that reveal the proportion of Negroes, both slave and free, to the total population between 1798 and 1888. Slaves worked as mine workers, as agricultural laborers, and in various capacities in the urban centers. The vast majority, however, was always employed on the sugar, cotton, coffee, and cacao plantations. Despite laws designed to protect the slave from cruel masters and overseers, the conditions under which farm workers labored were harsh.

Page 73, *Mitigating factors.* There was no law against teaching slaves to read and write in Brazil, therefore many became literate. By law, slaves had to be baptized within at least one year after their arrival in the country. After that, slaves were expected to attend mass and confession regularly. Another positive feature was the actual encouragement given to masters to manumit their slaves. Finally, it is generally agreed that in the colonial period Brazilians felt little, if any, racial prejudice.

Pages 73–75, *Resistance to slavery in Brazil.* From the beginning, black people registered their resentment against slavery by running away. At times, runaways organized into groups called *quilombos.* One of the most desperate bids for freedom came in the seventeenth century with the establishment of the black Republic of Palmares. Described as a remarkable political and economic achievement which grew from a handful of runaways into a complex political organism of many settlements, it took a number of military campaigns to finally defeat it. As elsewhere, resistance in Brazil resulted at times in violent and bloody insurrections.

Pages 75–80, *The abolition of slavery.* Haiti was the first of the New World states to abolish slavery, but legal freedom did not come to all blacks of the area until Brazil emancipated her slaves in 1888. Between 1794 and 1888 the slaves of Latin America gained their freedom. In both Spanish and Portuguese America the thrust for freedom was related to the struggle of colonies for their independence. The fact that both slaves and free blacks fought for the independence of the colonies gave impetus to the fight for the emancipation of slaves. With the achievement of independence, the fight for the abolition of slavery gained ammunition and converts.

Sentiment for abolishing slavery in the British possessions appeared in the eighteenth century in England. Note the *Somerset* case of 1772 in which the decision was made that slavery was too odious an institution to exist in England itself without specific legislation that sanctioned it. Pressure from organized British abolitionists, aided by favorable economic and military circumstances, led to the official closing of the slave trade in 1807. It was not until the year 1833 when, under continued and well-organized pressure from antislavery crusaders, a bill for the abolition of slavery was enacted.

This was a compensated emancipation, while for slaves a transition period from slavery to freedom was provided.

Despite opposition to emancipation by those who had invested heavily in slave property, emancipation in Latin America was not accompanied by the bitterness and hostility that it encountered in the United States. Respect for black people as human beings, their integration into the community's life, and the willingness of most Latin American owners to acknowledge the human depravity of slaveholding, all contributed to an acceptance of emancipation, with or without compensation to owners.

SELF-TEST

Multiple Choice

1. Which of the following mitigated the harshness of the institution of slavery in Spanish America?
   a. the influence of the Catholic church.
   b. the wide area over which a relatively large number of slaves was dispersed.
   c. a greater respect for Africans as human beings than there was in English America.
   d. all of the above.

2. The first European nation to sense the importance of African slave labor was:
   a. England.
   b. Spain.
   c. Portugal.
   d. France.

3. In colonial Brazil:
   a. the manumission of slaves was actually encouraged.
   b. the teaching of slaves to read and write was forbidden.
   c. the law required that all baptized slaves be set free within a year after baptism.
   d. the opportunity to purchase their freedom was denied to all slaves.

4. Three of the following regarding slavery in Spanish America are false. Which one is *true*?
   a. Slaves rarely, if ever, registered discontent with their lot.
   b. They were primarily agricultural workers.
   c. There was no comprehensive code that regulated slave activity.
   d. Control of slaves was left entirely up to local authorities.

Fill in the Blanks

1. _viceroyalty of New Grenada_ The largest concentration of blacks in continental Spanish America was to be found in the region comprising this governmental unit.

2. _Brazil_ Legal freedom did not come to all of the slaves of the New World until this country finally emancipated its slaves.

3. _asciento_ Contract granted to others by Spain for furnishing her colonies with slaves.

4. _Republic of Palmares_ Negro state established by fugitive slaves in northeastern Brazil from 1630 to 1697.

5. _Haiti_ The first of the New World countries to abolish slavery.

True or False

_T_ 1. Blacks in Spanish America were primarily agricultural workers.

_F_ 2. It is generally agreed that slavery in colonial Latin America was harsher than slavery in English America.

_F_ 3. Spaniards in colonial Spanish America showed a marked distaste for intermarriage with Negroes.

_F_ 4. The vast majority of slaves in Brazil were employed in urban areas as domestic servants.

_T_ 5. There was no law against the teaching of slaves to read and write in Brazil.

Essay Questions

1. Compare and contrast slavery as an institution in Latin America with slavery in English America.
2. Briefly comment on each of the following types of work engaged in by slaves in colonial Brazil: (a) urban tasks, (b) mining, (c) agricultural activities.
3. What were the chief characteristics of slavery in Spanish America? Can you see any similarities between the institution in Spanish and Portuguese America?
4. What similarities or differences can you see between the slave codes of the English American colonies and the codes of Spanish and Portuguese America?
5. Briefly, but adequately, comment on each of the following, giving the significance of each: (a) the *asiento,* (b) *quilombos,* (c) the Republic of Palmares.

Identify and/or Define

mitigate	*quilombos*	Thomas Clarkson
entrepôt	viceroyalty	William Wilberforce
Lebensraum	Toussaint L'Ouverture	

chapter VII

THAT ALL MEN MAY BE FREE

Chronology

1770	Boston Massacre: Crispus Attucks martyred
1775	In Philadelphia, Quakers organize first abolitionist society in America
1775	Enlistment of Negroes into continental armed forces forbidden
1775	Slaves invited to join British army in return for freedom
1776	Declaration of Independence adopted, after deletion of Jefferson's denunciation of slavery
1776–1778	Reversal of policy of excluding Negroes from service in America's armed forces

INTRODUCTORY STATEMENT

ENGLAND'S VICTORY in the French and Indian War (1756–1763) presaged a new imperial policy for her American colonies. Heavily in debt and confronted with pressing problems, the British government attempted to strengthen and unify its colonial system. Convinced that the colonists should contribute financially to the defense of the Empire, Parliament imposed new taxes which were met with immediate opposition. Significantly, some of the colonists linked the problem of slavery with their own fight against the mother country. Dramatizing the connection between the colonial conflict with Britain and the status of black people in the colonies was the martyrdom of the runaway slave Crispus Attucks, one of the first to fall in the Boston Massacre in 1770. Meanwhile, Negroes affected by the contemporary protestations of liberty, initiated suits for their freedom and sent petitions to the general assemblies of New England.

The War for Independence provided the slave with an opportunity to gain his freedom in exchange for service in the military forces. Despite the colonial policy of legal exclusion of blacks from military service, Negroes had frequently served in the wars against the French and Indians. This policy continued to be ignored in the early battles of the Revolutionary War. But shortly thereafter, a policy of excluding both slaves and free blacks from the state militias as well as from the Continental Army evolved.

Manpower shortages, which became evident as the war progressed, forced American leaders to rethink their exclusion policy. The need to permit blacks to fight was made more urgent by the action of the British in welcoming such enlistees in His Majesty's forces. The prospect of liberty prompted slaves to fight on both the British and American sides; thus Negroes fought not only for political independence, but for their individual freedom as well.

Even before the surrender of the British forces at Yorktown, the state of Pennsylvania had made provisions for the gradual abolition of slavery. By 1790, other northern states had abolished or were in the process of gradually manumitting their slaves. The passage of a gradual abolition law by New Jersey in 1804 sounded the death knell for slavery in the entire region. It should be remembered that the national government under the Articles of Confederation adopted the Northwest Ordinance of 1787 which, among other things, prohibited slavery in the area north of the Ohio River.

Opposition to the egalitarian program of social action began to appear after the war. One manifestation of this opposition was a hardening of resistance to an incipient movement to end the slave trade and abolish slavery. Conservative reaction culminated in the actions of delegates to the Constitutional Convention of 1787. Three of the provisions of the United States Constitution as ratified concerned slaves, even though the word itself does not appear. These concerns had to do with counting of slaves for purposes of representation and taxation; protection of the African slave trade for twenty years; and the obligation of states to permit masters to reclaim fugitive slaves. There were some among the delegates who felt, as did Oliver Ellsworth of Connecticut, that "slavery in time will not be a speck in our country." That his views were not shared by delegates from the South is clear from their successful efforts to have the institution of slavery sanctioned by the supreme law of the land.

STUDY NOTES

Pages 81–82, *Slavery and the Revolutionary philosophy.* Before 1763 there had been no frontal attack upon the institution of slavery, even in the northern colonies where there was no extensive use of slave labor. After this year American colonists seemed to realize the inconsistency in their position as oppressed colonists *and* slaveholders. Britain's attempts to strengthen and unify its colonial system, and its decision to impose new taxes on the colonists were met with stiff resistance. It is pointed out here that it was almost natural for the colonists to link the problem of Negro slavery to their fight against England. Meanwhile, Negroes themselves joined in the struggle for individual freedom through petitions to the General Court of Massachusetts on the grounds that freedom was their natural right.

Pages 82–83, *Crispus Attucks.* The martyrdom of Attucks is significant because his death dramatized the connection between the struggle against England by the colonists, and the depressed status of black people in colonial America.

Pages 83–85, *The Declaration of Independence*. Even though some colonists continued to speak against slavery and England at the same time, and to articulate the view that slavery was inconsistent with their struggle against England, delegates to the Continental Congress in 1776 were unwilling to see Jefferson's "philippic against slavery" become a part of the Declaration of Independence. Professor Franklin refers to this reaction as "the test of the colonists' regard for slavery." One part of the Declaration was a list of specific charges or grievances against the king. Among these harsh and uncompromising charges was one that placed the blame for a continuation of the slave trade and slavery on the monarch. Realizing that these accusations were unjust, the members rejected this charge and it was deleted from the final document. Furthermore, delegates who favored slavery realized that if this section was retained in the Declaration of Independence there would be no justification for the institution once independence was won. The point is made that the silence of the document on the matter of slavery and the slave trade was to make it equally difficult for abolitionists and proslavery leaders to look to it for support in the future.

Pages 85–87, *Negroes legally excluded from the fight for independence*. For various reasons, including the fear of slave insurrection, the official decision was made that black men, whether slave or free, would not be permitted to enlist as soldiers either in Washington's Continental Army or in the state militias. As early as May 1775, the significant conclusion was reached that the use of slaves as fighters would be "inconsistent with the principles that are to be supported." Despite the policy of legal exclusion some black men saw action in early battles of the conflict, and fought valiantly. The move to ban blacks entirely was dramatized by the attempt of Edward Rutledge of South Carolina, strongly supported by many of the southern delegates in the Continental Congress, to discharge all Negroes in the army. Although this effort failed, it was decided that no Negro, slave or free, would be permitted to enlist.

Pages 87–88, *Reversal of black exclusion pattern*. The length of the war, manpower shortages, and the action of the British in making blacks welcome in their ranks led to the eventual reversal of the policy of excluding Negroes from the Continental and state armed forces. The action of Lord John Murray Dunmore, royal governor of Virginia, was a key to the American decision to reverse its exclusion policy. On November 7, 1775, Lord Dunmore declared free all slaves "that are able and willing to bear arms" and join His Majesty's troops. This bid for blacks had the effect of liberalizing the military policy of the colonists toward blacks. States began to enlist both slaves and free Negroes, with only Georgia and South Carolina continuing to oppose the enlistment of black soldiers.

Pages 88–91, *Black fighters*. Approximately 5,000 black men served as soldiers or sailors during the Revolutionary War. They served in the Continental forces and in the ranks of states. In some instances, Negro enlistees received the same bounty as whites, while masters were given bounties as payment for the freedom of their slaves. The vast majority served in units made up primarily of white men, with the largest number of Negro soldiers coming from the North. Note that Negro patriots wanted human freedom as well as political independence. They translated this desire into petitions such as that of a group of Massachusetts slaves who, in January 1773, asked the General Court (assembly) of that colony to liberate them from slavery. This was only one among many such requests for individual freedom.

Pages 92–94, *The movement to manumit*. The egalitarian philosophy of the Revolutionary period did bring certain benefits to black people. A number of slaves gained their freedom as a result of military service, even though the freedom of other Negro soldiers did not go uncontested. Adherence to the philosophy prompted some owners to free their slaves. Individual opponents of slavery became more articulate, and antislavery and manumission societies became more widespread. Note the organization of the first society by Quakers in 1775. Added to actions of individuals was the movement by northern states to eliminate slavery from within their borders. On the federal level, under the Articles of Confederation, Congress included in the famous Northwest Ordinance a provision prohibiting slavery in the old Northwest Territory. This was the region bounded roughly by the Mississippi River, the Great Lakes, and the Ohio River. This area is now the states of Ohio, Indiana, Illinois, Michigan, and Wisconsin.

Pages 94–96, *Conservative reaction and the federal Constitution*. Reaction to a "horrid vision of disorder" conjured up by conservative American leaders after the war, coupled with strong opposition to the movement to liberate slaves, found expression in the behavior of delegates to the Constitutional Convention of 1787. Here the question of slavery became an important consideration. Compromises were made, and substantial concessions were made to the South. The problem as to how slaves should be counted for purposes of representation in Congress and taxation was solved with the adoption of the three-fifths compromise. Other concerns that were compromised had to do with the protection of the African slave trade for twenty years, and the obligation of states to permit masters to reclaim fugitive slaves. Note that the provisions of each of these articles are included in the text; it will be to your benefit to become familiar with the wording of each. With the adoption of a national Constitution that recognized and legitimized slavery, an era in the political history of the United States as well as in the history of Negro Americans had come to an end. The onus of slavery was now on the United States.

SELF-TEST

Multiple Choice

1. Its unacceptability to conservative members of the Continental Congress forced Jefferson to delete from the original draft of the Declaration of Independence a section that:
    a. declared all slaves independent.
    b. upheld the king's right to rule the colonies.
    c. in effect condemned slavery.
    d. asserted that all men were created equal.

2. Three of the following are true. Which one is *false*? Negroes served as soldiers during the Revolutionary War:
   a. with both American and British forces.
   b. with the Americans, before and after a period of legal exclusion.
   c. generally in integrated units.
   d. only on the side of the American patriots.

3. All of the following were black soldiers who distinguished themselves in battle *except:*
   a. Edward Rutledge.
   b. Prince Hall.
   c. Peter Salem.
   d. Salem Poor.

4. The three-fifths compromise of the Constitution:
   a. reconciled the interests of creditors and debtors.
   b. protected the African slave trade for a time.
   c. stipulated that fugitive slaves be returned to masters.
   d. provided for the counting of slaves for purposes of representation in Congress and taxation.

5. Which one of the following is *not* true of black soldiers who served the cause of independence?
   a. The majority were from the South.
   b. Their commanding officers were generally white.
   c. The majority were from the North.
   d. Most served in units made up primarily of white men.

Fill in the Blanks

1. __1763__ The significant year that marked the beginning of a new British imperial policy and a new approach to the problem of slavery on the part of the colonists.

2. __Georgia__ and __South Carolina__ These two states opposed the enlistment of Negro soldiers throughout the duration of the Revolutionary War.

3. __Boston__ *massacre* The killing of five Boston citizens by British soldiers in March 1770.

4. *Lord John murray* __Dunmore__ The royal governor of Virginia who offered freedom to slaves in return for service in British forces.

5. __Abigail Adams__ Wife of famous patriot and colonial leader who supported the concept of freedom for slaves.

True or False

___F___ 1. Since the bulk of the Negro population was in the South, the majority of black soldiers were from this section.

___F___ 2. The command of an all-black company was, at first, eagerly sought by most of the white officers.

___T___ 3. The vast majority of Negro soldiers served in units made up primarily of white men.

___T___ 4. There are many instances of Negroes serving in the navy during the War for Independence.

___T___ 5. Manumission and antislavery societies became more widespread after the Revolutionary War.

Essay Questions

1. What was the significance of the year 1763 in British-American relations? What connection can you see between this new imperial policy and the new approach to the problem of slavery on the part of the colonists?
2. In what significant respect was Jefferson's original draft of the Declaration of Independence changed? What forced the change?
3. a. Trace the emergence of a policy of excluding blacks from American military service during the War for Independence.
    b. Account for the subsequent reversal of this policy.
4. Three articles reflecting the conservative outlook on slavery were written into the federal Constitution. Summarize the provisions and account for the inclusion of each.
5. Briefly, but adequately, comment on each of the following, giving the significance of each:
    John Woolman
    Abigail Adams
    Peter Salem
    Crispus Attucks

Identify and/or Define

"benign" or
  "salutary neglect"
colonial
imperial
egalitarian

abolition
manumission
conservative
Continental Congress

Articles of
  Confederation
Northwest Ordinance
  of 1787

chapter VIII

THE TURN OF
THE CENTURY

Chronology

1787   Free African Society organized by Richard Allen and Absolom Jones in
        Philadelphia
1787   African Lodge No. 459, first black Masonic lodge in America, organized
        by Prince Hall in Boston
1790   First decennial national census taken
1793   Cotton gin invented by Eli Whitney
1794   Bethel African Methodist Episcopal Church organized and dedicated by
        Richard Allen in Philadelphia
1808   Federal prohibition on importation of slaves from Africa in effect
1815   Thirty-eight blacks taken to Sierra Leone, at his own expense, by black
        shipowner Paul Cuffe

INTRODUCTORY STATEMENT

C ENSUS FIGURES OF 1790 revealed demographic patterns that
would be followed by the black population in the United States for
decades to come. Already the vast majority of Negroes lived in the South
Atlantic states, even though the Middle Atlantic states had a substantial
black population, with the New England region having the fewest. The migration of slaves to the rapidly developing Southwest began a pattern that
became well established in the nineteenth century. Despite some opposition
to slavery, which had been given support by the Revolutionary War philosophy and certain negative economic factors, forces were already in operation
to fasten the institution of slavery on the country with greater permanency.

It was the Industrial Revolution, marked by technological changes in
the cotton-manufacturing process, that had the effect of strengthening
slavery in the southern part of the new nation. With the invention of the
cotton gin in 1793, many planters, especially in the lower South, turned
from other crops to cotton. Increased demand for cotton was accompanied
by an increased demand for Negro slaves. An important corollary to this
was the continuing flourishing of the African slave trade, even after its
official prohibition by federal law.

Ironically, a Haitian revolution helped to provide additional land for slave expansion in this country. Toussaint L'Ouverture, the black leader of this uprising against Napoleon Bonaparte, was at the height of his power when the French leader regained the Louisiana Territory. Napoleon's inability to crush Haitian forces completely led him to abandon his dream of an empire in North America and subsequently to sell Louisiana to the United States.

It had already become apparent to Negroes that they would have to act to secure for themselves a measure of dignity and fulfillment in an atmosphere calculated to keep them in a condition of subservice. To many, it appeared that if they were to enjoy the fruits of the American dream, it would be through their own separate, independent institutions. Thus, one result of this search for intellectual and spiritual independence was the creation or organization of separate, all-black avenues and media of self-expression.

STUDY NOTES

Pages 97–98, *The Negro population in 1790.* One sign of growth and permanence evident in the early years of the new United States was a continuously increasing population. Along with a total increase was the growth of the Negro population, which in 1790 was concentrated in the South Atlantic states. Even though slavery was declining in the Middle Atlantic states, and rapidly dying in New England, forces were already in operation to fasten slavery on the country with greater permanency. These same forces were to increase, at least temporarily, the importation of slaves from Africa.

Pages 99–100, *Slavery gains a new lease on life.* The coming of the Industrial Revolution with its insatiable appetite for cotton, the invention of the cotton gin, and the opening of new lands to cotton cultivation all conspired to fasten slavery on the South. The demand for cotton fiber to feed newly developed machinery led to a search for a variety of cotton that could be easily separated from the seed, and for the invention of a machine that could do this work. Some planters had already experimented successfully with a long, silky sea-island fiber that was superior to the short-staple variety whose seeds were difficult to separate from the lint. Climatic conditions, however, limited the area in which the superior sea-island variety would grow. Until a method of seeding the more abundant short-staple cotton was found, there would be no commercial expansion of cotton culture over the South. This was the problem facing southern planters in the year 1793. In that year, a young Yale graduate who had accepted a position in Georgia as a private tutor, heard of the difficulty of ginning cotton. In a short period of time, he had invented a satisfactory engine (gin). This machine, whose basic idea was so easy to copy, transformed southern agriculture. The invention of this device, and the opening of new lands to cotton cultivation, increased the demand for Negro slaves.

Pages 100–102, *Trouble in the Caribbean.* The inability of Napoleon Bonaparte to cope successfully with the rebellion against the French in Haiti, which was led by Toussaint L'Ouverture, had a great deal to do with the decision to sell Louisiana to the United States. Apparently Napoleon had envisioned a French empire with Haiti as a key point in the Caribbean and Louisiana a granary for the entire colonial empire. Thus the effect of events in Haiti on the course of American history was extremely important.

Page 102, *The problem of runaway slaves.* The problem of slaves escaping from plantations was made more acute by the rather free movement of blacks from the Caribbean who had escaped into the United States. One result of the possibilities inherent in this state of affairs was the enactment of the first fugitive slave law in 1793. Note the provisions of this law in your text. You might want to compare it with a later, more stringent fugitive slave act of 1850 (Chapter XII).

Pages 103–105, *Closing the African slave trade.* After several unsuccessful attempts to secure the enactment of a federal law making the African slave trade illegal, such a law was passed on March 2, 1807. To go into effect on January 1, 1808, it prohibited the importation to the United States of slaves from Africa. Note reasons given in the text for the illegal persistence of the trade for many years after the act's passage.

Pages 105–109, *Individual strivings for independence.* The hardening into permanence of the institution of slavery, along with the persistence of the African slave trade into the nineteenth century, left little room for optimism among American black people. The prospect that slavery would ever be abolished in the United States seemed dim indeed. In such an atmosphere some individual blacks became involved in a search for personal independence or identity through self-expression or in the economic realm. Among them were Jupiter Hammon, the well-known Phillis Wheatley, Gustavus Vassa, and Benjamin Banneker, perhaps the most accomplished black man of the early national period. One of the more interesting was the pioneer black colonizationist, Paul Cuffe, who, at his own expense, transported thirty-eight Negroes to Sierra Leone in 1815.

Pages 109–113, *Establishment of separate institutions.* The desire for a viable social and religious life of their own led groups of Negroes to forge their own separate organizations. These included such diverse institutions as schools and benevolent and fraternal societies. Perhaps of greatest importance to the black man was his church. Religious bodies formed in this period, such as the African Methodist Church, gave to him not only an opportunity to worship but also an opportunity to develop leadership. Such religious leaders as Richard Allen and Absolom Jones were also community leaders who held the respect of their peers. Rejected in their early search for integration into the political, social, and economic life of the nation, they had no alternative except to create institutions of their own. Professor Franklin concludes that, in the case of both individuals and institutions, it is significant that a considerable effort was made to share in the general development of the country and to contribute to its growth.

SELF-TEST

Multiple Choice

1. The Negro population in 1790:
   a. was concentrated in cities and towns.
   b. was essentially rural.

c. included no free black men and women.
d. numbered slightly more than a million.

2. According to the census of 1790, the vast majority of Negroes lived in the South Atlantic states. In which of the following was the largest number found?
   a. Georgia.
   b. South Carolina.
   c. Virginia.
   d. Maryland.

3. One of the notable results of the invention of the cotton gin and the extension of the area of cotton cultivation was the:
   a. impetus given to manufacturing in the South.
   b. rise of a movement to enslave all free blacks.
   c. decision by Congress to extend the period of the African slave trade.
   d. increased demand for Negro slaves.

4. An accomplished black man who was editor of almanacs and who served on the commission appointed to define the boundaries and lay out the streets of the District of Columbia was:
   a. Benjamin Banneker.
   b. Richard Allen.
   c. Paul Cuffe.
   d. Prince Hall.

5. The federal law that prohibited the African slave trade:
   a. seriously hampered efforts of the South to industrialize.
   b. was welcomed by southern cotton planters.
   c. was unenforced from the beginning.
   d. was rigidly enforced.

Fill in the Blanks

1. _BOSTON_ The only American city that reported no slaves in its population in 1790.

2. _Eli whitney_ Inventor of the cotton gin.

3. _Taussaint L'Ouverture_ Intrepid black leader of antislavery forces in Haiti.

4. _Free African society_ Black self-help society organized by Richard Allen and Absolom Jones in Philadelphia in 1787.

5. _Richard allen_ Founder of Bethel Church in Philadelphia, the first African Methodist Episcopal Church in the United States.

True or False

_T_ 1. The Negro population in 1790 was essentially rural.

_T_ 2. In the years immediately following independence, there was some reason to believe that slavery would deteriorate.

_F_ 3. Revolutionary activity in the Caribbean had little effect on the course of United States history.

_F_ 4. The federal law outlawing the African slave trade was enforced rigidly from the beginning.

_F_ 5. Results of the Industrial Revolution had little, if any, effect on economic activities in the United States.

Essay Questions

1. Account for the continued existence and growth, or expansion, of slavery in the early national period. Analyze the economic factors involved.
2. Show the connection between turn-of-the-century revolutionary activities in the Caribbean and the course of events in the United States.
3. How do you explain the failure to enforce the federal law prohibiting the African slave trade?
4. How do you account for the post-Revolutionary trend among black people of establishing separate, independent social institutions?
5. Identify and explain various avenues utilized by individual Afro-Americans in their search for independence in the post-Revolutionary period. Illustrate your answer with a sampling of those involved in this quest for self-respect.

Identify and/or Define

cotton gin	almanac	Andrew Bryan James
short-staple cotton	George Liele	Derham
Industrial Revolution		

chapter IX

THE WESTWARD MARCH

Chronology

1804–1806	Clark's slave York serves as liaison between Indians and members of Lewis and Clark expedition
1814	Treaty of Ghent ends War of 1812 on the basis of the status quo ante bellum
1815	Battle of New Orleans, in which black soldiers contributed substantially to American victory
1817	Mississippi admitted to the Union
1819	Alabama admitted to the Union. Admission of Mississippi and Alabama extended the area of cotton cultivation.

INTRODUCTORY STATEMENT

A FTER 1800, the land beyond the settled areas began to attract more settlers and to exercise a profound influence on American life. This frontier land rapidly became an influence in the evolution of the institution of slavery and, therefore, in the history of Negroes in the United States. The ideals of freedom, which were dominant on the frontier, succumbed before the powerful forces demanding slavery, especially in the region that is now the southern Gulf states. This area came to be a section of intensive cotton cultivation, the cotton kingdom based on slavery. If the frontier, with its abundance of available land, promoted democracy, it also encouraged the westward expansion of slavery.

Even though President Madison stressed Britain's violation of America's maritime rights in his war message to Congress, the War of 1812 was fought partly because of the desire of some American leaders to acquire more territory. It was clear that the acquisition of new lands, particularly Florida, would expand the area into which slavery could be extended. The coming of war gave to black Americans another opportunity to serve their country. As before, Negroes in search of independence joined the British forces.

The ratification of the Treaty of Ghent, which ended the war, made possible the acceleration of the westward movement. One result of this accelerated movement of population was the addition of new states to the

Union. One of the most important single factors augmenting the westward movement was the domestic slave trade.

The increased demand for slaves encouraged the illicit African trade, and prompted some to advocate openly the official reopening of the trade. Professor Franklin draws the significant conclusion that without slavery and the slave trade the westward movement on the southern frontier would have been unsuccessful.

STUDY NOTES

Pages 114–115, *Frontier influences.* The Industrial Revolution and the invention of the cotton gin determined the course of events on the American frontier. The greater portion of settlers from the Atlantic coastal states were committed to the institution of slavery and, when possible, brought their slaves with them. For the slave who was taken into the cotton kingdom of the Southwest, there was little of either democracy or the freedom that Professor Frederick Jackson Turner discovered on the frontier.

Pages 116–117, *Negro pioneers in the westward march.* Frequently overlooked is the fact that black Americans were also intimately involved in the process of "winning the West." These pioneers included men who were guides, hunters, trappers, traders, and those who served as interpreters in Indian-white relations.

Page 117, *The War of 1812.* Fought ostensibly to force Britain to respect maritime rights claimed by the United States, this war was also the result of "agrarian cupidity." New members of Congress, elected in 1810, from new states or frontier regions of old ones in a number of cases, advocated war with Britain. These "war hawks" were also expansionist in outlook and understood that a victorious war would encourage the extension of slavery, particularly if all of Florida could be acquired.

Pages 117–119, *Black fighters.* Black soldiers and sailors saw service with the United States forces in this conflict. The point is made that there seemed to be no serious objections to the Negro's service in the armed forces of the United States, but there was little inclination to recruit him. In some cases, slaves who enlisted with their master's permission were to receive their freedom at the war's end. Negroes served in both the army and navy, in a number of instances performing with gallantry. Note also the contribution made by Philadelphia's black citizens in helping to erect adequate defenses for the city. Pragmatic in his approach, the black man who saw a chance to gain his freedom by fighting on the British side did so.

Pages 120–121, *Emergence of the cotton kingdom.* The westward movement was accelerated by the War of 1812. Slavery flourished as the soil was exploited, and many land-hungry planters, with their slaves, deserted older regions of the South to push into the fertile lands of the Gulf region. Forces set in motion by the emergence of this kingdom largely account for the United States' acquisition of Florida and Texas. They also help to explain the reason for southern insistence on the entrance of Missouri into the Union as a slave state.

Pages 123–125, *The domestic slave trade.* Increased demand for slaves and the closing of the African trade by law represented a boon to states of the upper South who had slaves for sale. As a result it became the practice to purchase slaves in such states as Virginia and sell them in the lower South. In one sense, this internal trade was a supplement to the African trade. In your textbook the mechanics of this obnoxious business are described, along with references to some of the principal characters involved. The principal trading centers in the older and newer states are listed, with attention given to Washington, the nation's capital, as the "most notorious down to 1850" when the slave trade there was officially prohibited.

Pages 125–127, *Slave breeding and family separation.* Two of the uglier and most callous aspects of this sordid interstate trade were two practices engaged in systematically. One was the deliberate breeding of slaves, "one of the most fantastic manipulations of human development in the history of mankind." Despite state laws forbidding the practice, in the sale of slaves there was the persistent practice of dividing families. This was one of the most agonizing aspects in this traffic in human beings.

Pages 127–129, *Slave hiring.* For various reasons, some masters hired out their slaves for periods of time ranging from a day to a year. These hired hands engaged in work running the gamut from agricultural activities to service occupations in urban communities.

Pages 129–131, *Persistence of the African trade.* The prospect of huge profits in what seemed to be an insatiable market, along with the ease with which slaves could be smuggled into the United States combined to keep the trade open. Of prime interest is the fact that American citizens were the moving forces in this illicit traffic. In spite of the lax enforcement of the law, southerners who profited one way or another from the trade began to advocate openly the official reopening of the business.

SELF-TEST

Multiple Choice

1. One of the basic causes of the War of 1812 was:
    a. British efforts to end the slave trade.
    b. the desire of some American leaders to acquire more territory.
    c. the failure to resolve a boundary dispute between the United States and British Canada.
    d. the attempt on Britain's part to regain American lands lost in the Revolution.

2. During the War of 1812:
    a. blacks served in both the American army and navy.
    b. the British refused to allow black men to enter their ranks.
    c. black men were rebuffed by both sides.
    d. Andrew Jackson made Negroes unwelcome in the ranks of forces under his command.

3. All of the following practices were closely allied with the domestic slave trade *except:*
   a. slave breeding.
   b. dividing slave families.
   c. slave hiring.
   d. refusing to permit the interstate shipment of slaves.

4. Called the "very seat and center of the slave trade":
   a. Charleston.
   b. Memphis.
   c. the District of Columbia.
   d. New Orleans.

5. Which of the following represented the attempt to secure a supply of labor for work in the cotton kingdom?
   a. establishment of the domestic slave trade.
   b. illegal importation of slaves from Africa.
   c. only choice *a.*
   d. choices *a* and *b.*

Fill in the Blanks

1. _the frontier_ The Industrial Revolution and the invention of the cotton gin determined events on this outer edge of American settlement.

2. _James P. Beckworth_ Described as "the most intrepid and remarkable of the black explorers of the American West."

3. _war hawks_ Term applied to congressional advocates of war with Britain.

4. _war of 1812_ Black men fought on both sides in this conflict between Britain and the United States.

5. _Northwest ordinance_ Statute that prohibited slavery in the Old Northwest.

True or False

_F_ 1. There is no record of Afro-Americans participating in the exploration of the trans-Mississippi West.

_T_ 2. One of the most important single factors augmenting the westward movement was the domestic slave trade.

_F_ 3. Negroes served in the army but not in the navy in the War of 1812.

F 4. The extension of democracy was not a primary motive of any of the southern expansionists.

T 5. Closely allied with slave trading was the practice of slave hiring.

Essay Questions

1. The Industrial Revolution and the invention of the cotton gin were important considerations in determining the course of events on the American frontier. *Explain.*
2. Discuss the role of the black man as a participant in the War of 1812.
3. Write a brief but adequate essay on the domestic slave trade, paying attention to the reasons for its emergence and the mechanics of the trade.
4. Account for the persistence of the African slave trade into the nineteenth century, despite the federal law prohibiting it.
5. Comment on each of the following, giving the significance of each: (a) slave breeding; (b) slave hiring; (c) Manifest Destiny.

Identify and/or Define

frontier	prolificacy	John Melvin
war hawks	Manifest Destiny	Edward Rose
ubiquitous	Treaty of Ghent	Pierre and George
augment	Frederick Jackson	Bouga
impressment	Turner *a historian of frontier*	James P. Beckwourth

Map Study

Referring to the map that follows, use the following key to show:

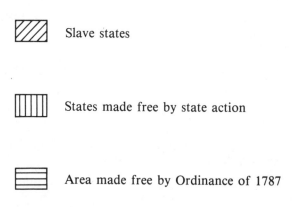

Slave states

States made free by state action

Area made free by Ordinance of 1787

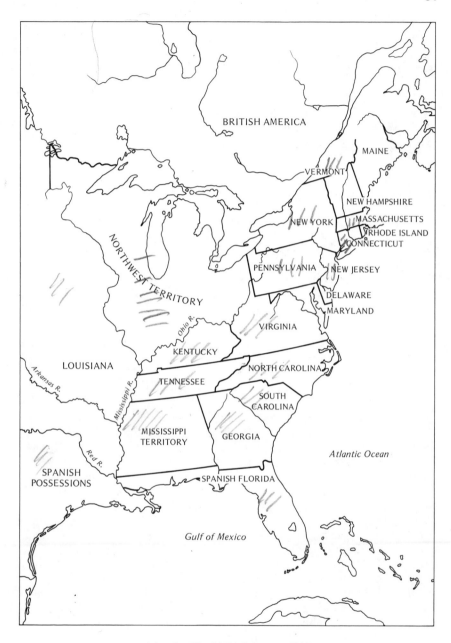

Map 2. The United States, 1800

chapter X

THAT PECULIAR INSTITUTION

Chronology

1800   Gabriel Prosser insurrection in Virginia
1822   Denmark Vesey insurrection in South Carolina
1829   Publication of David Walker's *Appeal,* an incendiary pamphlet which
       put South's nerves on edge
1831   Nat Turner insurrection in Virginia

INTRODUCTORY STATEMENT

EXTREMELY INFLUENTIAL in the economic and social life of the antebellum South was the development of cotton culture. This gave the region its most important staple crop and helped to preserve slavery. To the southerner, cotton cultivation seemed completely suited to servile labor. Few tools and little expensive equipment were needed in its production. Women, children, and men could be employed in the fields, compactly massed in gangs under the supervision of the owner or an overseer.

At the top of the social, economic, and political structure of the South were the great plantation owners. Their number was comparatively small, but the tremendous productivity of the large plantation units placed the large slaveholder in a position of disproportionate influence. Three fourths of the whites owned no slaves and had no direct economic interest in the institution. Wealth and power were in the hands of the planter oligarchy because of their large landholdings and ownership of slaves. As might be expected, there was always the hope on the part of nonslaveholders that they would someday become owners. As a result, this white majority assumed the habits and thought patterns of their wealthy and powerful neighbors. This largely accounts for their failure to condemn either the institution itself or the evils that were associated with it.

The maturing of the institution and the growth of the slave population were accompanied by new laws designed to insure protection of whites against any dangers that might arise from slave actions. Like their colonial counterparts, these state laws, or codes, were negative and repressive, aimed at regulating and restricting every aspect of the slave's life. Formal agencies of government as well as social institutions cooperated in the enforcement of these codes. Rigidly enforced during periods of revolt or when there were rumors of insurrection, the laws were observed with some degree of laxity during quiet times.

Slaves reacted in various ways to their lot. The docility with which many slaves conducted themselves was in reality a form of accommodation to a situation over which they had no control. Some probably took refuge in ritual and song. Other reactions that revealed dissatisfaction included feigning illness, self-mutilation, suicide, and running away. The most violent reaction of slaves was insurrection, the largest and most dramatic of which was the Nat Turner rebellion of 1831. This insurrection was savagely repressed and its leader was executed, but slaves continued to demonstrate their bitter antipathy to their condition of bondage throughout the antebellum period.

STUDY NOTES

Page 132, *The South's peculiar institution.* The exploitation of human and natural resources and the harsh discipline fostered by the growth of the big cotton plantations created a situation in the South different from the usual frontier experience. Slavery, gradually abolished in the North and excluded from the territory north of the Ohio River, survived and grew in the southern part of the United States to become the region's "peculiar institution."

Pages 133–134, *Extent of slave ownership.* The slave population was concentrated in the hands of a relatively few white southerners, of whom 88 percent could be considered small slaveholders; that is, the bulk of the slaves were owned by small farmers. However, the tremendous productivity of the large plantations placed the large slaveholder in a position of disproportionate influence. It should be remembered that the majority of slaveholding was carried on by yeomen rather than by gentry.

Pages 134–136, *To control a "troublesome" property.* The growth of slavery was accompanied by the enactment of new and stringent laws to regulate and control the lives of all slaves. Repressive and regulatory, these codes aimed at protecting whites against slave revolt or any other dangers that might arise from the presence of large numbers of blacks. Control of the slave was exercised not only through the formal machinery of government and devices responsible to the government, but through such social agencies as the church. Note restrictions imposed by the codes and machinery that was provided for enforcement and execution.

Pages 136–138, *Work on the plantation.* The majority of slaves were agricultural workers, with the bulk of this number employed on cotton plantations. On the large plantations there were generally two distinct types of workers, the house servants and the field hands. Note description and contrasting duties or tasks engaged in by both groups. Depending on the crops raised, one of two work systems was used—the "task" system or the "gang" system. These two are described in the text.

Pages 138–141, *Treatment of the slave.* In an effort to get work out of slaves, who understandably felt no compulsion to extend themselves, the lash was frequently used. The naive or sinister racial justification for this was that Negroes were members of a childlike race and should be punished just as children were. The greatest cruelty and brutality existed on plantations supervised by overseers, whose chief concern was to produce a superior crop. In spite of the rigors associated with their work, slaves were generally inadequately fed and poorly housed, and they were furnished with no more clothing than was absolutely necessary.

Pages 141–142, *Nonagricultural pursuits.* A sizable number of slaves lived in urban communities throughout the antebellum period. These slaves were engaged in a variety of occupations. The majority found employment as domestic servants, porters, or common laborers in the towns, while others labored in construction camps outside the town. In the face of disapproval from white skilled workmen, a significant number of slaves worked as artisans.

Pages 143–145, *Social considerations.* Slaves had little "free" time for recreation, particularly after they had reached the "useful age." Two periods when work activities eased somewhat were the summer lay-by time and Christmas. Religious activities were encouraged as a useful form of indoctrination. This meant that separate black churches and congregations, with their own preachers or leaders, were frowned on and their services restricted. Blacks were required to attend white churches; this permitted whites to keep a "closer eye" on their slave communicants.

Pages 145–147, *Educational opportunities limited.* Teaching slaves to read and write was against the law. Some masters violated the law with impunity, or simply ignored it, by instructing selected slaves personally. Scattered here and there were some Negro schools, and in some isolated cases blacks were permitted to attend school with white children.

Pages 147–149, *The slave family.* Seldom recognized as a basic social institution worthy of respect, it was extremely difficult for the slave family to maintain itself on a stable basis. Stable slave families emerged where elements calculated to insure permanence in marriage were present. The slave woman was frequently forced to bear children by the venality of her master. In such cases the family status was quite tenuous. All too often slave women were subjected to the sexual whims and desires of white men. Children born of these unions were slaves, whose white fathers might reject completely, or, unwilling to see them remain slaves, might emancipate them and provide for their well-being.

Pages 149–153, *The slave's reaction to his status.* Even though slave-owners attempted to convey the impression that their slaves were docile, tractable, and happy, in most cases the evidence does not support this contention. The slave adopted techniques of adjustment to his depressed status, concealed his feelings very effectively, and in various ways revealed his opposition to his state of servitude.

Pages 153–156, *Slave insurrections.* Conspiracy to revolt and actual rebellion were the most dramatic and desperate reactions of slaves to their status. These manifestations of resistance to bondage were present in the colonial period and persisted until 1865. Actual revolts and possibilities of insurrection kept southerners apprehensive throughout the antebellum period. Note examples given in the text. Two things bear mentioning: one is that, at times, blacks warned their white masters of planned uprisings thus betraying the black leaders of planned revolts; another is the encouragement and assistance that in some cases whites gave to black conspirators. How does the author of the text explain this action on the part of whites?

SELF-TEST

Multiple Choice

1. In 1860, three fourths of the white people of the South:
   a. owned twenty or more slaves.
   b. had neither slaves nor an immediate economic interest in the maintenance of slavery.
   c. were operators of large plantations.
   d. favored the immediate abolition of slavery.

2. Of the states having slaveholders with more than twenty slaves, this state led the rest:
   a. Alabama.
   b. Georgia.
   c. Mississippi.
   d. Louisiana.

3. Slave codes expressed the point of view that:
   a. slaves were not persons but property.
   b. laws should protect the ownership of slave property.
   c. whites should be protected against possible slave rebellion.
   d. all of the above were essential.

4. It was generally believed that:
   a. one slave was required for the cultivation of three acres of cotton.
   b. each slave should be given a specific work assignment or task each day.
   c. house servants were more valuable than field hands.
   d. slaves should never be exposed to any form of religious activity.

5. The invitation to Negroes to attend white churches:
   a. represented a movement in the direction of Christian brotherhood.
   b. was never extended in the South.
   c. provided an opportunity for blacks and whites to worship in an integrated setting.
   d. was a method that whites employed to keep a closer eye on the slaves.

Fill in the Blanks

1. _Planters_ Although in the minority, this class of southerners exercised a disproportionate amount of influence.

2. _Slave codes_ Restrictive laws that deprived slaves of virtually all civil, judicial, political, and familial rights.

3. _Summer Layb^l_ and _Christmas_ Two periods to which slaves could look as times of recreation.

4. _Patrol_ Described as an adaptation of the militia to maintain slavery, it assisted in the enforcement of the slave codes.

5. _Gang_ Plantation slaves labored generally under the "task" or "gang" system. Under which did the majority work?

True or False

_F_ 1. A majority of southern whites owned slaves.

_F_ 2. By law, an owner was forbidden to work in the fields with his slaves.

_F_ 3. Owners generally selected their overseers from the slaveholding class.

_T_ 4. Some slaves lived and worked in urban communities.

_T_ 5. Despite legal restrictions, some slaves were taught to read and write.

_F_ 6. The singing slave was a happy and contented slave.

_T_ 7. Housing for slaves was especially poor and inadequate.

_F_ 8. Most white artisans welcomed skilled black workmen into their ranks.

_T_ 9. The southern church came to be used as an agency for maintaining slavery.

_T_ 10. The cotton plantation was the typical locale of the slave.

Essay Questions

1. a. Show briefly how cotton and slavery dictated the economic and social development of the antebellum South.
   b. Why were nonslaveholding whites interested in maintaining slavery?
2. a. Differentiate between classes of slaves, indicating the primary responsibilities of each.
   b. Give selected examples of nonagricultural pursuits engaged in by slaves.
3. a. Account for the emergence of the slave codes.
   b. To what extent were fears of slave revolts justified?
4. a. To what various means did slaves resort in reacting to their servile condition?
   b. The most sensational and desperate reaction of slaves to their status was the conspiracy to revolt. Explain.

5. a. Why was it difficult for the slave family to maintain itself on a stable basis?
   b. How do you account for the presence of mulattoes in the slave population?

Identify and/or Define

antebellum	gentry	artisan
yeoman	cabal	inveterate

chapter XI

QUASI-FREE NEGROES

Chronology

1802   Free blacks legally excluded from the franchise in Washington, D.C.
1817   American Colonization Society formed January 1
1826   Edward Jones (Amherst) and John Russwurm (Bowdoin), first American
       blacks to graduate from college
1827   Samuel Cornish and John Russwurm began publication of *Freedom's
       Journal,* first Negro newspaper
1847   The African Methodist Episcopal Church began publication of *The
       Christian Herald;* name changed to *Christian Recorder* in 1852

INTRODUCTORY STATEMENT

F REE PERSONS OF color, especially those in the antebellum South, represented an American anomaly, constituting as they did a third element in a social system planned for two. The existence of a body of free blacks early came to be regarded by the whites as a menace to desirable social arrangements. As a result, this class was the object of constant attention and a considerable amount of restrictive state legislation. For those who lived in the free states and had to face economic and social proscriptions, there were compensations. Restrictions were not as severe, and because they had more of the law on their side, free Negroes could legally resist encroachments on their rights. Given greater opportunity for self-expression, black people organized and fought for what they conceived to be their best interests. Furthermore, they had a substantial group of white allies who gave them moral and material support.

By terms of the Northwest Ordinance, slavery was excluded from the territory north of the Ohio River; states north of Maryland and Delaware had abolished slavery by 1804, and the Missouri Compromise of 1820 provided that it would not exist in the Louisiana Purchase territory north of 36°-30'.

There were mixed reactions to the presence of free blacks in both the North and South. Many whites, and, for a while, some blacks felt that Afro-Americans should be deported. Advocates of colonization, preferably in Africa, were variously motivated. Some felt that the presence of free persons of color constituted a menace and that their removal would solve the problem. To others, colonization meant fulfillment of a moral obligation to return blacks to their African homeland. Some blacks reasoned that only in Africa or elsewhere could they realize their full potential' as men. The movement to colonize culminated in the founding of the American Colonization Society in 1817. This organization established the Republic of Liberia on the west coast of Africa as a place to which black people of the United States would be sent. By and large, however, Negroes themselves showed no desire to be deported. In the North, for various reasons, there arose almost universal opposition to colonization.

STUDY NOTES

Pages 157–159, *Rise and growth of the free Negro class.* The free Negro group originated with those who had completed their terms of indentured servitude in colonial times. Despite southern opposition to the presence of free persons of color, white persons were frequently responsible for the former's increase. Many slaves became free through acts of manumission by their masters, while other masters permitted their slaves to earn enough money to buy their freedom. Note other methods or ways by which the size of the class increased, for example, children born of free mothers were free from birth.

Pages 160–161, *Legal status in the South.* Free blacks lived upon the sufferance of the whites. Their conduct was regulated and their freedom of movement restricted by law. Kept under constant surveillance, they were required to carry on their persons certificates of freedom, and were compelled to register with state courts. In practically every southern state the law provided that free Negroes have white guardians, and that these Negroes have little contact with slaves. Such legal controls mounted year by year.

Pages 161–163, *Economic and political restrictions.* Even though required to work and keep their means of support visible, numerous types of occupations were closed to free blacks. By the end of the antebellum period practically every state had excluded them from the franchise. In New York, a property qualification of $250.00, along with a residence requirement of three years, effectively limited their participation in political and civic affairs. In states where they were not legally disfranchised their political influence was hardly noticeable.

Pages 163–166, *Economic development.* In the face of economic proscriptions it was difficult for this class as a whole to achieve stability and independence. The vast majority found employment as agricultural workers, as common laborers, or in service-related occupations. Urban free Negroes who were skilled workmen found greater opportunities to ply their trade in the more impersonal atmosphere of towns and cities. Some became affluent through the accumulation of real and personal property. Fewer still became owners of slaves. It should be understood that most Negro slaveholders had a personal interest in their human property, as for example, the case of an affluent free Negro who had purchased a relative in order to rescue the individual from the worst features of the institution of slavery.

Pages 166–167, *Social considerations.* The free Negro family was formed by marriage within the group, by marriage to slaves, or through legal or clandestine relations with whites and Indians. In the Deep South particularly there was little in the way of organized recreation for the group. In some areas, they found an outlet through fraternal organizations and benevolent societies.

Pages 168–171, *To worship and to learn.* The author of the text points out that important to the free Negro, as to the slave, was the church. Religious services provided opportunities for social intercourse as well as spiritual uplift. These opportunities were proscribed in the South, however, between 1820 and 1860. Free black preachers came to be suspected as possible instigators of trouble, and the separate, unsupervised congregations were seen as breeding grounds for antiwhite conspiracies. Opportunities for learning were greater in the North and West than in the South. Even in the North, however, separate schools were maintained, and in the Northwest there was generally an attitude of indifference to the problem of public school education for blacks. Note that Negroes made a start in higher education with blacks graduating from a number of colleges. In this connection, become familiar with Edward Jones and John Russwurm.

Pages 171–173, *Self-expression.* A cadre of articulate blacks emerged during the antebellum period. They expressed themselves through poetry and prose and as editors of independent newspapers. The largest and, in the opinion of Professor Franklin, perhaps the most significant group of Negro writers were ex-slaves who cited their experiences in narratives. Frequently these accounts were ghost-written by white abolitionists, but some were the genuine work of ex-slaves such as Frederick Douglass, who had received the rudiments of an education. An important medium of expression was the black newspaper. As might be expected, most of the Negro papers were concerned mainly with the antislavery crusade. Blazing the trail for a long line of black newspapers was *Freedom's Journal,* first published in 1827.

Pages 173–175, *Obstacles in the North and West.* All too often, free blacks outside the South were the victims of a pervasive feeling of hostility from white citizens. This feeling of antagonism was manifested, at times, in physical violence. Note that sometimes this violence reached the proportions of riots in such states as New York, Pennsylvania, and Ohio. In their favor was the fact that in the North free blacks could legally resist encroachments on their rights with, at times, the active assistance of white allies.

Pages 175–176, *The convention movement.* This movement, which began around the year 1830, functioned throughout the antebellum period. Organized and attended by prominent black leaders, these national conventions had as their general aim the improvement of conditions among members of the free black group.

Pages 176–179, *Colonization.* One method advanced as a "solution" to the "problem" posed by the presence of Negroes in America was physical removal to some place outside the country. The organization of the American Colonization Society culminated the organized movement to deport black people. In spite of fairly widespread approval by prominent white individuals as well as by state legislatures, the raising of thousands of dollars, and the establishment of Liberia in Africa, the movement ultimately failed. Of the reasons for its lack of success, a primary one was the opposition of the great majority of black people themselves. It should be noted that a relatively small number of black leaders did support colonization, but they remained in the minority.

SELF-TEST

Multiple Choice

1. One provision of the Ordinance of 1787 prohibited slavery in the:
   a. New England section.
   b. Middle Atlantic states.
   c. Northwest Territory.
   d. Louisiana Purchase territory.

2. Census figures reveal that this state led all others, with 83,900 free blacks in 1860:
   a. Virginia.
   b. Maryland.
   c. Pennsylvania.
   d. New York.

3. The existence of a large group of free persons of color in the South was a source of constant concern to slaveholders because:
   a. all free Negroes were the natural offspring of white persons.
   b. the majority of free blacks owned slaves.
   c. all free Negroes were guilty of inciting slave revolts.
   d. their presence tended to undermine the very foundation on which slavery was built.

4. Despite the organized effort to colonize free blacks, not more than this number migrated:
   a. 1,420.
   b. 30,000.
   c. 10,000
   d. 15,000.

5. The first black newspaper published in the United States was:
   a. *Freedom's Journal.*
   b. *North Star.*
   c. *Colored Man's Journal.*
   d. *Anglo-African.*

Fill in the Blanks

1. _Free_____ The legal status of children born to free mothers.

2. _North Star_ The name of the newspaper when it was first published by Frederick Douglass in 1847.

Christian Herald

3. _____ In 1847, the African Methodist Episcopal church began publication of a weekly magazine under this name.

American colonization society

4. _____ This organization had as its purpose the colonization of free black people.

Certificate of

5. *Freedom* _____ Most southern states required free Negroes to carry this document on their persons at all times.

True or False

F 1. The free Negro class had its origin in the post-Revolutionary period.

T 2. Some slaves were able to gain their freedom through self-purchase.

T 3. Free Negroes tended to be city dwellers.

F 4. Unlike the slave, the free black had unlimited freedom of movement.

F 5. Manumission carried with it civil and political rights as well as legal freedom.

T 6. The right to own property and dispose of it was generally conceded to free persons of color.

F 7. Their hatred of slavery explains the absence of slaveholding among free Negroes.

F 8. Racial animosity in the North forced Negroes in that section to totally support colonization.

T 9. National conventions provided northern blacks with one means of articulating their concerns.

T 10. A child born to a slave father and a free mother was free from birth.

Essay Questions

1. Account for the origin and increase in the number of antebellum free Negroes.
2. a. By what means did southern state legislatures attempt to keep free blacks under surveillance?
   b. What other controls proscribed the activities of the group?
3. How can you explain the ownership of slaves by free Negroes?
4. a. What various motives help to explain the founding of the American Colonization Society?
   b. Why did it eventually fail?
5. What was the "essential difference" for the Negro between the South and other regions? Show how this difference was reflected in the convention movement.

Identify and/or Define

quasi
sufferance
clandestine
quadroon
surveillance
franchise

proscription
disesteem
affluence
anomaly
Lunsford Lane
Solomon Humphries

James Forten
John Chavis
William Wells Brown
William C. Nell
Martin R. Delany

chapter XII

SLAVERY AND INTERSECTIONAL STRIFE

Chronology

1829   David Walker's *Appeal,* calling on slaves to revolt, published
1831   First issue of William Lloyd Garrison's militant antislavery *The Liberator* published
1833   American Antislavery Society organized in Philadelphia by white and black abolitionists
1850   Compromise of 1850 enacted by Congress
1852   Harriet Beecher Stowe's *Uncle Tom's Cabin* published
1854   Republican party organized
1857   Dred Scott decision handed down
1859   John Brown's raid at Harpers Ferry, Virginia
1860   Abraham Lincoln elected President

INTRODUCTORY STATEMENT

T HE AUTHOR MAKES the point that the antislavery sentiment generated by humanitarians in the eighteenth century never completely died out in America. This sentiment, however, found little continuing adherence in a South increasingly committed to an agrarian civilization in which servile labor came to be regarded as essential for economic and social development. The contest over the admission of Missouri into the Union heightened already existing sectional tensions. The issue in this controversy of 1819–1820 was primarily economic and political, with little attention being paid to the moral aspects of slavery. However, as some leaders of public opinion began to speak out openly against slavery, both in the South and the North, attention became focused on the evils of the institution. Their approach to the elimination of slavery was moderate and found expression in a number of antislavery newspapers published in the South. This program of gradualism, with compensation to owners and colonization of freed blacks, gave way in the 1830s to a more militant, uncompensated type of immediate abolition. Confined to the North, it was the most significant aspect of a larger contemporary humanitarian movement. From the beginning, black abolitionists were conspicuous in the movement to end slavery in this nation. As would be expected, in the face of the militant abolitionist onslaught southerners adopted a positive defense of their peculiar institution, and the South became a bastion of proslavery thought.

Although the status of slavery was settled in the Louisiana territory by the Missouri Compromise, it became a problem in the territories acquired from Mexico. Various policies with regard to slavery in the Mexican cession were advanced, none of them entirely satisfactory. In an attempt to settle the whole question of slavery, including the matter of fugitive slaves, Congress enacted the compromise measures of 1850. In the end this effort failed, but it did postpone the resort to arms. One political result of the stress and strain engendered by the disputes of this decade was the formation of the new Republican party, which was opposed to the further extension of slavery.

When the Supreme Court injected itself into the slavery controversy with the Dred Scott decision, it made a peaceable solution even more difficult. The two last important links in the chain leading to the "irrepressible conflict" were John Brown's raid in October 1859, and the election of the "Black Republican," Abraham Lincoln, in 1860. Shortly thereafter South Carolina seceded from the Union, to be followed by other Deep South states. Thus, it was the question of slavery more than any other sectional issue that sundered the Union and led to a bloody Civil War.

STUDY NOTES

Page 180, *Sectional division after 1816.* The North gained unity through manufacturing, with the region's factories being staffed with free labor. The South remained basically an agricultural section, deriving its chief income from staple crops and the plantation system. The people of the area increasingly came to feel that perpetuation of the institution of slavery was essential to its way of life.

Pages 180–181, *The gradual abolitionists.* Antislavery sentiment appeared early in America, went through a period of quiescence, and began to increase after 1815. Moderate and conciliatory in tone and approach, opposition to slavery was expressed in the pages of antislavery newspapers published by Quakers in the South for several years.

Pages 181–182, *Arrival of the age of militant abolitionists.* Three events are said to have ushered in the age of the militant abolitionists. These were the publication of David Walker's *Appeal* in 1829; the first appearance of William Lloyd Garrison's newspaper, *The Liberator,* in 1831; and the insurrection of Nat Turner in the same year, which many southerners connected directly to the activities and pronouncements of men like Garrison. Walker's incendiary pamphlet was at once a scathing denunciation of slavery and a militant invitation to slaves to revolt and throw off the yoke of slavery. In the first issue of *The Liberator,* the editor made it clear that he was not a moderate in his approach to liberation, that he would not equivocate, and that he would be heard as a most articulate spokesman of the cause.

Pages 182–183, *The antislavery argument.* These two pages of the text present the chief postulates developed against the perpetuation of slavery. You might want to construct a chart with these in one column, and the postulates of the proslavery defense in another. Note that both sides could use arguments that were basically similar but manipulated in such a way as to support completely different conclusions.

Pages 183–186, *Mechanics of the antislavery crusade.* The fight against slavery became an organized movement, beginning with the formation of the New England Anti-Slavery Society in 1831. After a schism between Garrisonians and others stemming from differences as to tactics and strategy to be employed, effective work was done by state and local organizations. Those who had faith in the political process organized the Liberty party in 1840 and in two successive presidential campaigns offered a candidate for that office. It should be clear that, even in the North, there was always some sentiment against abolition, or against certain tactics supported by the more militant abolitionists. This opposition frequently became violent, as was demonstrated in the mob killing of the abolitionist editor Elijah P. Lovejoy.

Pages 186–189, *Black abolitionists.* From the beginning of the movement black people were prominent in the crusade to end slavery. Negroes were active in formal antislavery societies and served in official capacities. They gave their time, energy, and money to national as well as to local and regional societies. They wrote and spoke out against slavery, at times with militant bitterness. The outstanding black abolitionist was Frederick Douglass, whose lectures against slavery were delivered not only in the United States but in England as well. His newspaper, the *North Star,* whose name was changed in 1850 to *Frederick Douglass' Paper,* became an influential medium through which his views could be disseminated.

Pages 189–194, *The Underground Railroad.* An organized, systematic effort to undermine slavery, this was the means by which a large number of slaves were assisted in making their way out of the South to the free states or to Canada. Operated mainly at night, the Railroad's operatives were adept at smuggling runaways into the North.

Pages 195–199, *The proslavery argument.* In the face of the abolitionist attack, the South began to strike back at its tormenters. In time an elaborate defense of slavery was worked out. This proslavery argument was based on the specious theory of the racial inferiority and biological inequality of black people. The South became a closed society in which there was no room for either free speech or free inquiry.

Pages 199–204, *Stress and strain in the fifties.* The decade of the fifties was filled with tense and crucial moments, the majority of which were connected with the question of slavery. To be more exact, the question of the extension of slavery into the recently acquired territories occupied a great deal of the attention of Congress as well as that of the citizens of both the South and the free states. Sharply differing opinions and beliefs as to the status of slavery in the new areas, and the extent of the power of Congress to exclude the institution from the territories caused controversy and bitterness. It was in this tense atmosphere that such acts of Congress as the Compromise of 1850 and the Kansas-Nebraska Act of 1854 appeared. Adding fuel to strained intersectional relations was the novel *Uncle Tom's*

Cabin published in 1852. The decision in the case of *Scott* v. *Sanford* (the Dred Scott case) convinced many northerners that the Court was in league with southerners in a plot to extend slavery into the territories, and widened the breach between North and South. The two last "links" in the chain of events leading to the Civil War were John Brown's seizure of the federal arsenal at Harpers Ferry, and the election of Abraham Lincoln as President in 1860. Shortly after Lincoln's election, the state of South Carolina seceded from the Union. As you ponder this action, remember that he had not been an avowed abolitionist.

SELF-TEST

Multiple Choice

1. Militant abolitionists demanded:
   a. only that Congress forbid the further extension of slavery.
   b. immediate abolition of slavery with no compensation to owners.
   c. gradual emancipation and colonization for freedmen.
   d. immediate abolition with owner compensation.

2. Which one of these was *not* a major southern defense of slavery?
   a. black people were inferior and destined for a subordinate position.
   b. the Bible sanctioned slavery.
   c. slavery was unprofitable and if let alone would rapidly die out.
   d. slave labor was an economic necessity to the South.

3. Which part of the Compromise of 1850 did the South find most acceptable?
   a. the admission of California as a free state.
   b. the provision that certain territories be organized without mention of slavery.
   c. a stringent fugitive slave law.
   d. the abolition of the slave trade in the District of Columbia.

4. The election of 1860 brought to the presidency:
   a. one who advocated reopening the African slave trade.
   b. an opponent of the further extension of slavery.
   c. a man highly acceptable to southerners.
   d. a militant abolitionist.

5. The Underground Railroad operated:
   a. in violation of federal fugitive slave laws.
   b. generally in broad daylight.
   c. its lines only in the North.
   d. without the assistance of any black operators.

Fill in the Blanks

william L. Garrison

1. _____ The most articulate spokesman of nonviolent militant abolition.

2. <u>American Anti-slavery Society</u> Organized in 1833, its members were committed to a crusade for the immediate abolition of slavery.

3. <u>Liberty Party</u> Political party that, in the presidential elections of 1840 and 1844, demanded the abolition of slavery.

4. <u>Gale rule</u> Name given to the action of the House of Representatives that, from 1836 to 1845, denied Americans the right of petition.

5. <u>underground Railroad</u> Organized effort to undermine slavery by assisting runaway slaves escaping from the South.

True or False

__F__ 1. Militant abolitionists supported the idea of financial compensation to owners of freed slaves.

__F__ 2. Abolitionists pointed out that slavery was contrary to the teachings of Christianity.

__T__ 3. Militant abolitionists were, on the whole, opposed to colonization.

__F__ 4. Black men spoke in favor of emancipation but were not permitted to support it in print.

__T__ 5. Lincoln won the election of 1860 primarily because of his substantial electoral vote from the South.

Essay Questions

1. Account for and discuss analytically the militant abolitionism of the 1830s and subsequent years, comparing this phase with earlier movements to abolish slavery.
2. Compare and contrast the reaction of southerners and northerners to the militant antislavery crusade, including in your answer both the antislavery and proslavery arguments.
3. React to this statement: The average white northerner was willing to tolerate slavery where it already existed, but unwilling to see it spread into free areas of the nation. In this connection, what was the significance of the novel *Uncle Tom's Cabin*?
4. Relate the following to the slavery controversy and the coming of the Civil War.
   a. Compromise of 1850
   b. Kansas-Nebraska Act
   c. Dred Scott case
   d. John Brown's raid
5. Make a concise statement about the Underground Railroad. Include in your discussion a brief description of its operation.

Identify and/or Define

Benjamin Lundy
William Lloyd
 Garrison
Theodore Weld
Elijah P. Lovejoy

James G. Birney
Lewis Tappan
Prudence Crandall
Harriet Beecher
 Stowe

John Fairfield
Henry Highland
 Garnet
Harriet Tubman
Henry Box Brown

Map Study

Referring to the map that follows, use the following key to show:

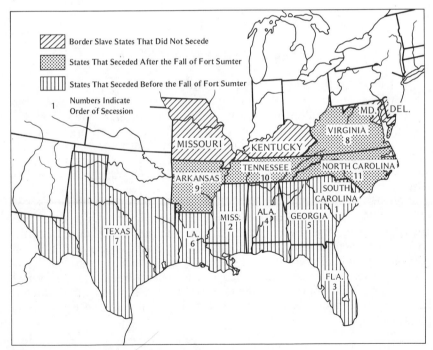

Slave states and territories

Free states and territories

Map 3. Slave and Free Territory, 1850

ReFer To MAP on Page 75

chapter XIII

THE CIVIL WAR

Chronology

1861   Bombardment of Fort Sumter by Confederate forces (April)
1861   Confiscation Act enacted by Congress (August)
1862   Preliminary Emancipation Proclamation issued by President Lincoln
1863   Emancipation Proclamation in effect, January 1
1863   Draft Act enacted by Congress (July)
1863   Draft riots in New York City (July)
1865   Surrender of Confederate forces at Appomattox

INTRODUCTORY STATEMENT

P RESIDENT LINCOLN'S declaration in August 1861 that his primary objective in the Civil War was "to save the Union" and "*not* either to save or to destroy slavery" affirmed a war aim widely shared by northern whites. Preservation of the Union, not abolition of slavery, was the stated goal of the Lincoln administration. This attitude, distasteful as it was to black people and abolitionists, gradually gave way to a more humanitarian goal. The freeing of the slaves was a significant result of the war.

When Lincoln called for volunteers after the bombardment of Fort Sumter, Negroes were prominent among those who rushed to offer their services. Their offers were rejected, and for the first eighteen months blacks were denied permission to enlist in the armed forces of the Union. Despite continuing opposition of many northern whites to arm blacks and permit them to wear uniforms, the exclusion policy had to be abandoned. The length of the conflict and the need for more manpower led not only to a change in Union policy but to the active recruitment and use of black fighting men.

Slaves and free blacks were pressed into the service of the Confederacy as laborers. This kind of assistance was welcomed, but to arm blacks and ask them to fight was quite another thing. Reverses in the field and manpower shortages combined to produce enough of a change in official thinking so that by March 1865, the Confederate Congress provided for the recruiting of slaves to be used as soldiers. By this time the war, to all intents and purposes, was over.

The two most significant results of Union victory were the restoration of the Union and the end of chattel slavery. The war itself hastened the overthrow of the landed oligarchy and transferred economic and political power to the rising financiers and industrialists of the nation.

STUDY NOTES

Pages 205–206, *The coming of war.* President Lincoln's decision to hold and defend Fort Sumter and its consequent bombardment by Confederate forces plunged the nation into its Civil War. As you consider his moderate and conciliatory inaugural address, remember that some slave states had not yet acted to leave the Union. As you analyze the President's war policy, also remember that four slave states remained loyal to the Union. The desirability of keeping these states in helped to dictate policy as it affected black people, to a far greater degree than was pleasing to either Negroes or abolitionists. This also helps to explain why blacks were excluded at first from service in the armed forces.

Pages 206–210, *The Union government and the Negro.* Professor Franklin correctly characterizes federal policy concerning black people at the beginning of the war as "uncertain" and "vacillating." Supporting this description is the lack of uniformity in the matters of relief and employment to slaves who poured into Union lines as the federal armies moved into the South. The question of the disposal of fugitive slaves, as a practical matter, was at first handled by the commanding officers in the field. Uniform treatment had to wait until the enactment of the Conscription Act by Congress in August 1861. The lack of a uniform federal policy for relief of freedmen prompted private agencies to emerge and to render aid. Private organizations also made significant contributions toward the education of freedmen.

Pages 210–212, *Reversal of the exclusion policy.* Despite continued opposition from articulate segments of the northern white population to the black man's utilization as a soldier, the policy of bypassing him had to be abandoned. The length of the war and the consequent need for more manpower led to the official decision to enlist Negroes. Even before the official policy was enunciated, General David Hunter, Commander of the Department of the South, had made an abortive attempt to organize an all-black regiment. Meanwhile, hostile feelings toward blacks which were encouraged by the irresponsible journalism of antiadministration newspaper editors, fear of job competition from freed Negroes, and resistance to being drafted, help to explain the New York draft riots of 1863.

Pages 212–214, *Lincoln, Congress, and the Negro.* Lincoln's views on emancipation included gradual emancipation with financial compensation to owners, and subsequent removal of the freedmen from the United States. During the war, laws were passed that liberated slaves in the District of Columbia and abolished slavery in the territories. Another law set free all slaves escaping from disloyal masters into Union-held territory. However, the President was unsuccessful in his efforts to persuade masters of slaves in the loyal border slave states to accept any plan for compensated emancipation.

Pages 214–216, *The Emancipation Proclamation.* By the summer of 1862, President Lincoln had moved to the point of seriously considering emancipating, by proclamation, all slaves in the rebellious states. Against the advice of a majority of his Cabinet he decided to issue such a proclamation. Union success at Antietam on September 17, 1862, furnished him with the military excuse for such an action. In that same month he issued a preliminary proclamation that gave to the rebellious states time in which to act on their own. The southern states ignored his warning. When the time arrived, he issued the final Emancipation Proclamation which declared free all slaves in states or parts of states still in rebellion against the United States on January 1, 1863. You should observe that Lincoln justified his action as a "fit and necessary war measure" for suppressing rebellion "as an act of justice, warranted by the Constitution upon military necessity." As an "act of justice" the Proclamation won friends abroad, and as a war measure it created confusion in the South. You should also observe that the states or parts of states affected were those areas over which the Union armies had no control. Slaves in the loyal slave states were not affected. You should realize, however, that with the issuance of this document, the war to preserve the Union had given way to a war to expand the area of human freedom. Note reaction to this action, both in the North and abroad.

Pages 216–221, *Confederate policy.* Some historians refer to the peaceful devotion of the slaves during the war. This was true of some, but unquestioned devotion and loyalty to the master class was the exception rather than the rule. The southerner moved to tighten controls over the slave and to make running away even more difficult. In spite of this there was a wholesale exodus of slaves into the nearest Union lines. In various other ways slaves made it clear that they preferred freedom to bondage. Confederate and state governments made use of slaves and free blacks in prosecuting the war. It was not until the waning days of the conflict, however, that the Confederates made the momentous decision to arm slaves and permit them to serve in the Confederate military forces.

Pages 221–224, *Black soldiers.* One policy for the future laid down in the Emancipation Proclamation was that of using black men as soldiers. This sanction led to systematic enlistment of black troops. Unfortunately, the first of these were discriminated against in pay and treatment. In the face of this discrimination, black soldiers performed valiantly, seeing action in every theater of operation during the war. Note that the mortality rate among black troops was substantially greater than that among white soldiers, and the reasons why. Aside from the dangers faced by others, the black soldier had to face a "no-quarter" policy established for him by the Confederates. You will see that this policy helps to explain the excessively high mortality rate among black soldiers.

Pages 224–226, *Union victory.* Two important immediate results of the war were the end of slavery and a preserved Union. Forces set in motion ushered in an economic revolution that transformed America.

SELF-TEST

Multiple Choice

1. Abraham Lincoln:
   a. favored total and immediate emancipation of slaves.

b. supported unconditional abolition without compensation to owners.

c. wanted gradual emancipation with compensation to owners.

d. opposed the idea of colonization of freed slaves outside the United States.

2. The Emancipation Proclamation:

   a. represented the first official action taken with regard to slaves.

   b. liberated slaves in all slaveholding states.

   c. was enthusiastically received by northern whites.

   d. was justified as "a fit and necessary war measure."

3. When black men first offered their services as soldiers to the Union, they:

   a. were permitted to enlist, but their pay was less than that of whites.

   b. had to sign up for the duration of the war.

   c. were rejected.

   d. were accepted, but assigned to all-black units.

4. Three of the following are false. Which is *true*?

   a. the South used Negro troops from the beginning of the war.

   b. the North eventually used black soldiers.

   c. both the North and South enlisted a substantial number of black soldiers.

   d. neither side ever contemplated the arming of black men.

5. Which of the following represented acts of slave disloyalty to masters during the Civil War?

   a. deserting to Union lines.

   b. refusal to work or submit to punishment.

   c. seizing the master's property when the chance presented itself.

   d. all of the above.

Fill in the Blanks

1. _Maryland_ Four slave states remained loyal to the Union. Three of them were Delaware, Kentucky, and Missouri. Which was the fourth?

2. _confiscation act_ This measure of Congress (1861) was the first official step taken in the direction of providing "uniform treatment" for fugitives who took refuge behind Union lines.

3. _American missionary association_ Religious organization that demonstrated early its interest in education for black people.

4. _David hunter_ High-ranking Union army officer who activated the short-lived "First South Carolina Volunteer Regiment."

5. _54th massachusetts regiment_ This military unit served a year without pay rather than accept the discriminatory wages at first paid to black soldiers.

True or False

T 1. Lincoln felt that the war was justified as a means to preserve the Union.

T 2. The escape of slaves to Union lines raised an early problem as to their legal status.

F 3. The Emancipation Proclamation abolished slavery as an institution.

T 4. Negroes eventually saw action in every theater of the Civil War.

F 5. From the beginning, black soldiers received the same pay and treatment as did white soldiers.

Essay Questions

1. Account for the opposition of northern whites to the emancipation of slaves during the war. How do you relate this negative attitude to the white workers' resistance to the Draft Act of 1863?

2. Describe Lincoln's program for "solving the problem" of black people in the United States. In what vital respects did it differ from that of abolitionists?

3. Analyze the Emancipation Proclamation as both a "war measure" and a "humanitarian" move. In your analysis show Lincoln's justification for it; identify the areas directly affected by it; and comment briefly on the general reaction to the issuance of the proclamation.

4. a. In what various ways did slaves demonstrate their dissatisfaction with their status during the war?
   b. How did slaveowners and government officials attempt to maintain the status quo?

5. Write a brief essay on the black man in the Civil War, tracing the evolution of an official policy with regard to his use as a soldier.

Identify and/or Define

vacillation
confiscate
excoriate
contraband
exodus
impressment
mortality rate
"running the
Negroes"

Robert Smalls
Horace Greeley
Rev. L. C.
   Lockwood
Mary S. Peake
General Lorenzo
   Thomas

Fort Pillow affair
The Planter
American Missionary
   Association
Battle at Antietam
   Creek (1862)

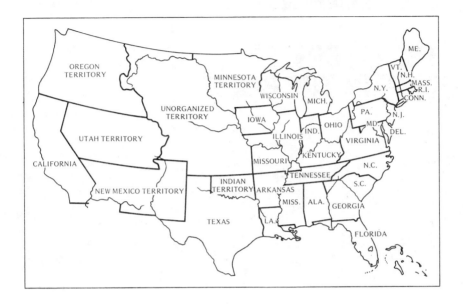

Map 4. The Process of Secession

chapter XIV

THE EFFORT TO ATTAIN THE PEACE

Chronology

1863   Proclamation of Amnesty and Reconstruction issued by President Lincoln. Basis for his ten percent plan of Reconstruction

1324   Wade-Davis bill represented opposition of some Congressmen to Lincoln's lenient plan

1865   Bureau of Refugees, Freedmen, and Abandoned Lands established by Congress (March)

1865   Freedmen's Savings and Trust Company chartered by Congress. Bank's business confined to blacks.

1865   Thirteenth Amendment passed by Congress (January)

1867   First Reconstruction Act passed by Congress. Basis for congressional plan of Reconstruction

1868   Fourteenth Amendment

1870   Fifteenth Amendment

INTRODUCTORY STATEMENT

T HE CIVIL WAR resolved two important controversies: It ended chattel slavery and permanently established the ultimate supremacy of the national government. On the other hand, the war created problems, not just for the South but for all sections of the nation. Perhaps the greatest effect of the conflict was the stimulation that it gave to industrial growth in the North. Along with this came the growing power of industrial capitalism and the rise in political importance of the northern business and financial leaders. Even before the war, the Republican party had allied itself with northern industrialists, and this alliance became stronger in the postwar years. The party sponsored protective tariffs, aided railroads, opposed inflation, and aided industrial capitalism. Growing interest in these areas was accompanied by a lessening of concern for the freedmen on the part of Congress and the North. It is necessary to understand this in order to assess properly what went on in the South between 1865 and 1876, as well as the direction taken by the nation after the settling of the disputed presidential election of the latter year.

Thus, Reconstruction was not simply a southern phenomenon but an integral part of the nation's history. Most citizens were affected by problems following the war, but it was the freedman who was the target of much attention and ultimately the victim of the postwar chaos. In the South an entirely new political structure had to be erected out of the wreckage left by war, with consideration given to the new rights and duties of the freedmen. Two separate and distinct policies of reconstruction were tried. The first followed the beliefs and ideas of Presidents Lincoln and Johnson. This presidential plan encountered much opposition from Congress and was eventually defeated.

The congressional plan, which replaced that of President Johnson, provided for the active participation of black men in the drawing up of new state constitutions and in the political process of each of the reconstructed southern states. Erected after Negro suffrage was instituted, these so-called Radical Republican governments were administered by a coalition of whites and blacks. Despite assertions to the contrary, these governments were at no time ruled by illiterate blacks.

During the years after 1867, black people benefited from the widespread interest in their education and rehabilitation. This interest was transformed into action by private organizations as well as by the federal government. The adoption of the Fourteenth and Fifteenth amendments to the United States Constitution represented attempts to write into the supreme law certain safeguards for America's black citizens. It is unfortunate that in succeeding decades the intent of these amendments was either circumvented or ignored.

STUDY NOTES

Pages 227–330, *Reconstruction and the nation.* In these pages the author makes it clear that Reconstruction was a national problem, rather than merely a sectional or southern problem. It was not simply a story of "Negro rule" or "southern history." To be understood, Reconstruction must be studied in its national setting.

Pages 229–330, *The South and the problems of the freedmen.* Among the immediate postwar problems was that of economic rehabilitation. Other pressing problems were the restoration of seceded states to their place in the Union and, extremely important, the role of the black man in this process. In solving these problems it was essential to try to replace sectional bitterness with a new spirit of conciliation and goodwill.

Pages 230–231, *Presidential policies and the "10 per cent plan."* President Lincoln assumed that the war had been basically a rebellion of citizens who had misled their state governments, rather than a revolt of the states. This led him to conclude that Reconstruction was an executive matter, to be dealt with solely by the President. As early as December 1863 he issued a Proclamation of Amnesty and Reconstruction. This was the basis for the "10 per cent plan," generally approved in the North. Some states reorganized themselves under its provisions, but it aroused opposition from the Radical Republicans of Congress. Feeling that the plan was too lenient and that Reconstruction should be handled by Congress, they enacted a more severe measure of their own. This Wade-Davis bill, which Lincoln felt was too severe, was pocket-vetoed by the President. Contrast its provisions with those of the Lincoln plan. Significantly, the freedman's right to vote or hold public office was not provided for in either plan.

Pages 232–233, *Action by Congress.* Shocked though they were by the assassination of President Lincoln, Radical leaders had reason to feel, or at least felt so, that Andrew Johnson would make a more pliant President. They were pleased when he called for complete abolition of slavery, repudiation of Confederate war debts, and the nullification of the ordinances of secession. His continued lenient approach to Reconstruction, however, along with his attitude that this was a matter for the President alone to handle, soon aroused their displeasure. Actions of the southern states reconstructed under the presidential plan convinced many northerners that the South was trying to undo certain important results of the war. Their refusal to enfranchise blacks, their insistence on sending former prominent Confederate leaders to Congress, and the enactment of Black Codes which seriously restricted the civil and economic rights of black people exasperated northern members of Congress. Led by such friends of the freedmen as Charles Sumner and Thaddeus Stevens, Radical Republicans prevented the seating of the newly elected southern representatives. A Joint Committee on Reconstruction was created to investigate the claims of these new states for recognition. The first open break between Johnson and Congress came when the President vetoed a bill extending the life of the Freedmen's Bureau. To answer the Black Codes and to guarantee civil rights to blacks, Congress passed the Civil Rights Act of 1866. Vetoed by Johnson, it was passed over his veto, marking the first time in United States history that a major enactment of the Congress became law over the President's veto. Other actions of President Johnson added fuel to congressional discontent and deepened the split between the two.

Pages 233–234, *Congressional plan of Reconstruction.* Acting on the report of the Joint Committee on Reconstruction, Congress denied to the southern states the privilege of statehood until certain guarantees were written into the Constitution and agreed to by these states. There was a strong feeling that the main features of the Civil Rights Act should be incorporated into an amendment. Out of this conviction came the Fourteenth Amendment. Section 1 of this amendment conferred citizenship upon Negroes and forbade any state to abridge the privileges or immunities of citizens or to deprive any person of life, liberty, or property without the due process of law. The southern states, with the exception of Tennessee, rejected the amendment. Failure of these states to ratify and Johnson's repudiation at the polls in the fall elections of 1866 cleared the way for Reconstruction on terms established by Congress. The provisions of the Reconstruction Act of 1867 are spelled out in the text. Contrast this approach to Reconstruction to that of the President, noting that the act was passed over Johnson's veto. Some scholars have felt that much of the controversy surrounding this phase of Reconstruction would have been avoided had Lincoln not been assassinated, given Lincoln's skill at handling men and Johnson's ineptness and obstinacy. On the basis of what you have read this far, can you venture an opinion of your own? The author refers to a "coalition of interest" which triumphed in the victory of Congress; could Lincoln have been more successful than Johnson in coping with this diverse group?

Pages 234–238, *Relief and rehabilitation.* In the summer and fall of 1865, when the state governments established under the presidential plan of Reconstruction held sway, blacks meeting in state conventions gave vent to frustration at being denied the rights of full citizenship. Their protestations were ignored in the South, but the Bureau of Refugees, Freedmen, and Abandoned Lands (Freedmen's Bureau), and private organizations with similar aims were at work in their behalf. The Freedmen's Bureau has been described as a protective agency organized to aid and guide the black man in his transition from slavery to freedom. Active in many areas, it proved helpful to many freedmen, but in the process it aroused the hostility of native southerners. The Bureau achieved its greatest success in education and cooperated with northern philanthropic and religious organizations in the opening of many schools. The black church was also a significant source of both spiritual and material relief, and its influence was reflected in an increasing membership.

Pages 238–240, *Economic adjustment.* Adjusting economically to a condition of freedom proved difficult for many blacks. As might be expected, most southern blacks found work in agriculture. Even though they were paid only a pittance in wages, or were simply allotted a share of the crops they raised along with lodging, most freedmen did find work. The author points out that black farm workers contributed greatly to the economic recovery of the war-ravaged South. Unfortunately for the workers, though, the South generally recovered much more rapidly than did the former slaves. Although they were not given "40 acres and a mule" by the federal government, some freedmen did secure homesteads that could be used as the base for a stable economic life.

Pages 240–242, *Organized labor, business enterprise, and the Negro.* Unsophisticated in the ways of the organized labor movement, the black laborer became a pawn in the hands of unscrupulous manufacturers and entrepreneurs who used him to undermine white unions. This led to a feeling on the part of the white union member that the black worker was a poor union risk and consequently should be kept outside the movement. Little success attended the efforts of blacks to achieve economic independence through various forms of business enterprise. The author concludes that "perhaps the greatest failure of Reconstruction was economic."

Pages 242–244, *Political currents.* Some historians have referred to the period of Radical Reconstruction as a "tragic era" in which illiterate former fieldhands controlled the statehouses and courthouses. The period has been characterized as an abnormal one of rampant corruption, when southern state treasuries were robbed by venal carpetbaggers, scalawags, and their ignorant black pawns. While not denying that there was corruption and malfeasance in office, more scholarly estimates of the era point to the positive accomplishments of the state governments. Many black officeholders were far from being illiterate and conducted the affairs of their offices with integrity and efficiency. State constitutions drawn up by integrated conventions are described as "the most progressive the South had ever known." Many of their provisions were retained by the conservative southerners after they regained control of, or "redeemed" their states. It can be denied, with solid evidence, that there was any "carpetbag rule" in the commonly used sense of that term.

Pages 244–248, *Black officeholders.* During the period of Radical

Reconstruction black men held public office in the states of the former Confederacy They sat in the legislatures and held many offices of lesser influence at the local level. At no time was a black man elected governor, although in South Carolina, where blacks wielded the greatest influence, there were two lieutenant governors. Three black lieutenant governors served in Louisiana, with one of that number serving for a brief time in 1873 as acting governor. In most states black elected officeholders were neither larger in number nor inordinately influential. Black men also represented their states in the United States Congress, with two serving in the Senate and twenty in the House of Representatives between 1869 and 1901. By and large, black officeholders were efficient and conducted the affairs of their office with integrity. The author makes the point that "the graft and corruption of the period were neither new nor peculiar to the South." He makes it equally as clear that the graft and corruption should be seen in the perspective of the age. Read this section with care.

SELF-TEST

Multiple Choice

1. With regard to former slaves, the Freedmen's Bureau did all of the following *except:*
   a. provide them all with 40 acres of land and a mule.
   b. furnish supplies and medical services.
   c. supervise work contracts between freedmen and employers.
   d. establish schools.

2. The Bureau achieved its greatest success in the area of:
   a. economic rehabilitation.
   b. education.
   c. religious uplift.
   d. political participation.

3. One basic reason why Radical Republicans in Congress broke with Johnson was:
   a. resentment toward him as a former big slaveholder.
   b. his leniency toward the defeated South.
   c. his pressure on them to produce the Fourteenth Amendment.
   d. his advocacy of universal Negro suffrage.

4. An early blunder committed by the South was the:
   a. repealing of the Black Codes.
   b. creation of the Freedmen's Bureau.
   c. rejection of the Fourteenth Amendment.
   d. strong opposition to Johnson's policies.

5. Lincoln's "ten per cent plan:"
   a. granted citizenship to ten percent of the former slaves.
   b. was designed to restore control in the South to high former Confederate officers.
   c. was the same as provisions of the Wade-Davis Bill.
   d. offered amnesty to many southerners.

6. From which group did southern states choose their representatives while being reconstructed under the Johnson plan?
    a. former Confederate leaders.
    b. Freedmen's Bureau agents.
    c. poor whites.
    d. carpetbaggers.

7. One immediate result of the congressional plan of Reconstruction was the:
    a. denial of civil rights to former slaves.
    b. dissolution of the Freedmen's Bureau.
    c. active participation of blacks in southern politics.
    d. disfranchisement of the freedmen.

8. Between 1869 and 1901, which of the following black men served in the Senate of the United States?
    a. Edward Brooke and Robert Smalls.
    b. Francis L. Cardozo and Alonzo J. Ransier.
    c. John R. Lynch and J. T. Walls.
    d. Hiram R. Revels and Blance K. Bruce.

Fill in the Blanks

1. _thirteenth amendment_ This amendment to the national Constitution prohibited slavery in the United States.

2. _Black codes_ These southern state laws so restricted the civil and political rights of the freedman as to reduce him to a position of serfdom.

3. _freedmens bureau_ A protective agency established by Congress March 3, 1865, that aided and guided the freedman in his transition from slavery to freedom.

4. _Francis L. Cardoso_ This educated and talented Negro was South Carolina's secretary of state from 1868 to 1872, and the state's treasurer from 1872 to 1876.

5. _Fourteenth_ A serious blunder committed by southern states being reconstructed under the Johnson plan was their refusal to ratify this amendment.

True or False

_F_ 1. Reconstruction is best understood as a history of Negro rule confined to the postwar South.

_T_ 2. The question of the Negro was inseparably connected with the problems of Reconstruction.

___F___ 3. Lincoln's refusal to act without prior congressional approval complicated the problems.

___T___ 4. During Reconstruction, after 1867, black men held public office in the southern states.

___T___ 5. State governments reconstructed under the presidential plan refused to extend the franchise to black men.

___F___ 6. Southern officials, unwilling to concede the end of slavery, strenuously objected to the Thirteenth Amendment.

___T___ 7. The Freedmen's Bureau was hindered in its task by southern hostility and inefficiency among its own officials.

___F___ 8. The Black Codes reflected the willingness of southerners to recognize the former slave as a full citizen.

___F___ 9. Most of the blacks in Congress were illiterate former field hands with no prior experience in public service.

___T___ 10. The largest number of Negroes elected to the U.S. House of Representatives was sent by South Carolina.

Essay Questions

1. a. What two important controversies did the Civil War resolve? *Explain.*
    b. What immediate and far-reaching problems became apparent in the period after the war? *Why?*
2. Account for two separate plans of Reconstruction being placed in operation in the South, and describe the basic provisions of each.
3. Show clearly why the Reconstruction plans of Lincoln and Johnson failed. What actions of the South contributed to this failure? What blunders were committed by Johnson that led to conflict between himself and Congress?
4. In what ways did the Freedmen's Bureau come to grips with the needs of freedmen in their transition from slavery to freedom? Evaluate the success of this federal agency in solving problems.
5. Argue for or against the proposition that between 1868 and 1876 governments of the former Confederate states were ruled by illiterate, venal blacks who, through extravagance plunged these states into huge and unnecessary debts.

Identify and/or Define

choleric	Thaddeus Stevens	National Labor
venal	Wade-Davis bill	Union
despondent	Joint Committee on	Thirteenth
protagonist	Reconstruction	Amendment
vagrancy	Freedmen's Savings	Fourteenth
wily	and Trust	Amendment
Charles Sumner	Company	Fifteenth Amendment

chapter XV

LOSING THE PEACE

Chronology

1870–1871	Enforcement Acts designed to prevent intimidation of black voters by Ku Klux Klan
1875	Civil Rights Act, prohibited discrimination in public places and on public carriers
1875	*United States* v. *Cruikshank.* Supreme Court decision nullified intent of Fifteenth Amendment
1883	The Supreme Court outlaws the Civil Rights Act of 1875
1896	*Plessy* v. *Ferguson.* Supreme Court decision gives constitutional sanction to "separate but equal" doctrine

---

INTRODUCTORY STATEMENT

T HE PROBLEM OF establishing peace on a basis satisfactory to all was made more difficult by the conflicting views and goals of both the North and the defeated South. The still young Republican party was understandably determined to strengthen its position and to perpetuate its power. As the "respectable" party of the period, it could stigmatize the Democratic party as the party of treason and disunion. Desire to maintain its power helps to explain the willingness of many Republicans to enfranchise the freedmen, making certain that they became loyal Republican voters.

As conservative southern whites saw their political influence waning and their control of the freedmen lessening, they counterattacked, all too often resorting to violence. Extralegal, coercive organizations, some in existence before 1868, launched a campaign of terror designed to frighten blacks out of politics and to perpetuate white supremacy.

Home rule returned to the South gradually as southerners in one state after another "redeemed" their right to govern. In the process, it was made clear to black men that their newly won right to the franchise met with disapproval by local whites. Continued violent actions drove the point home. In the late nineteenth century state laws were passed that effectively disfranchised the Negro and reduced him to a political nonentity. Except for a short time when the Populist party sought his vote and vied with southern Bourbons for his support, the black man as a political force became impotent. Along with this deprivation of voting rights came the institutionalization of segregation. This movement culminated with the decision of the Supreme Court in *Plessy* v. *Ferguson,* which gave constitutional sanction to the "separate but equal" doctrine.

STUDY NOTES

Pages 251–255. *The struggle for domination.* The Republican party controlled the executive and legislative branches of the government in the postwar years. Supported by northern industrialists, by former Union soldiers, and by those who would protect the freedmen, it was also the "respectable" party of this period. The determination of many Republicans to stay in power helps to explain the motives of some who adopted the cause of black people. It made good political sense to enfranchise black men and to train them to vote for the party of Lincoln. Assisting in this crusade to enlist freedmen as Republicans were various groups. The chief recruiting agency was the Union League. When the freedmen, under Radical Reconstruction, voted almost solidly for candidates of the party, southerners resorted to violence in an effort to regain control of the freedmen. The violence culminated in the Ku Klux Klan movement. Only one of a number of extralegal terroristic secret societies that emerged in these years, the Klan became the best known and most infamous. Local efforts to suppress these types of outlaw organizations were generally ineffectual. Congress undertook to suppress them, with a greater degree of success, in a series of laws passed in 1870 and 1871. This struggle in the South was essentially a battle for political control of the region. The black man became the hapless victim when the Republicans, in their efforts to retain control, ran head-on into determined attempts by conservative local Democrats to "redeem" their states.

Pages 255–258, *The overthrow of Radical Reconstruction.* As southerners gradually recovered their voting rights and the privileges of citizenship, more and more native-born conservative whites returned to political power. With this rise in power came a revival of the Democratic party in the region. By 1876, every former Confederate state had been "redeemed" except Florida, Louisiana, and South Carolina. In the redemption process, intimidation and terrorism were employed freely to prevent black men from voting. In addition, the North finally "grew weary of the crusade for the Negro." Compounding the plight of black people were certain decisions of the United States Supreme Court that nullified the intent of voting rights legislation and the Fifteenth Amendment.

Pages 259–263, *The movement for disfranchisement.* The return of southern Democrats to political power meant that they could find or devise ways to prevent the black man's participation in state and local politics. Continuing to rely heavily on intimidation, they resorted to more sophisticated tactics also designed to nullify the political strength of blacks. Where Negroes were still voting, means were found to control their votes. A careful reading of these pages will reveal the statutory techniques by which blacks were disfranchised and the Fifteenth Amendment circumvented. For a brief moment in the latter part of the nineteenth century, a coalition of black and white farmers working through the Populist party showed promise of political resurgence for black southerners. But as the Negro regained a measure of political influence, conservative resentment against his participation in the political process grew even stronger. With the collapse of the farmers' revolt, the white South united in a movement for complete disfranchisement of the black man.

Pages 263–266, *The triumph of white supremacy.* To eliminate the possibility that white factions would compete with one another for the black vote and thus give the balance of power to black voters, Negroes were completely disfranchised. Beginning with Mississippi, southern states wrote guarantees of white supremacy into their state constitutions.

SELF-TEST

Multiple Choice

1. To understand the politics of the Reconstruction period, the student should become familiar with:
   a. the determination of Republicans to strengthen their position and perpetuate their power.
   b. the pressure of industrialists for favorable legislation.
   c. conflicting philosophies of Reconstruction.
   d. all of the above.

2. Radical Republicans supported:
   a. the extension of the franchise to the Negro, for altruistic *and* political reasons.
   b. stringent enforcement of a literacy test as a prerequisite for voting.
   c. a plan to abolish the Freedmen's Bureau.
   d. all of the above.

3. In the popular movement to disfranchise blacks, all of the following were employed *except:*
   a. the use of violence.
   b. refusal to permit Negroes to vote for candidates of the Democratic party.
   c. the practice of stuffing ballot boxes.
   d. changing the location of polling places without notification on Election Day.

4. In the movement to disfranchise blacks completely through legal means, the South used as prerequisites to voting:
   a. the "grandfather clause."
   b. payment of a poll tax.
   c. the ability to read or interpret the Constitution.
   d. all of the above.

5. Which one of the following did *not* support the Republican party's postwar goal of building a strong southern wing of the party?
   a. Freedmen's Bureau officials.
   b. Knights of the White Camelia.

    c. the Union League of America.

    d. missionary groups and teachers from the North.

Fill in the Blanks

1. _____ A protective and benevolent, but political organization, it was the most active agency in the recruitment of Negroes in the postwar South for the Republican party.

2. _____ In the year 1871, Conservative Democrats returned to political power in this state.

3. _____, _____, _____ The only states of the former Confederacy that remained under Republican control by the year 1876.

4. _____ In this case the Supreme Court held that the Fifteenth Amendment did not guarantee citizens the right to vote, but only the right not to be discriminated against by the state on account of race, color, or previous condition of servitude.

5. _____ In the late nineteenth century the southern wing of this political agency of farmers supported, for a brief time, the right of black men to vote.

True or False

_____1. Reconstruction ended abruptly as the result of official action from Washington.

_____2. By 1876 the North had grown weary of the crusade for Negroes.

_____3. The movement for disfranchisement of blacks was aided by the use of intimidation and violence.

_____4. One of the long-range results of Radical Reconstruction was the emergence of the "solid South."

_____5. Decisions of the Supreme Court had the effect of postponing the overthrow of Radical Reconstruction.

Essay Questions

1. Trace the movement to institutionalize the disfranchisement of blacks in the South after the return to power of Conservative Democrats. In your answer differentiate between extralegal and legal devices employed. Explain how disfranchisement was achieved in spite of the Fifteenth Amendment.

2. Differentiate between the purpose of the Union League and that of the Ku Klux Klan. Show how each operated to achieve its goal.
3. Comment on the role of the Populist party in black-white political relations in the South from 1892 to 1896.
4. How do you account for the ultimate failure of Radical Reconstruction in the South?
5. Comment briefly on and give the significance of each of the following:
   a. The Enforcement Acts of 1870–1871
   b. *United States* v. *Cruikshank*
   c. "Jim Crow" laws
   d. *Plessy* v. *Ferguson*

Identify and/or Define

altruistic	habeas corpus	Isaiah Montgomery
perfidy	hapless	Thomas E. Miller
catechize	gerrymander	James Wigg

chapter XVI

PHILANTHROPY AND SELF-HELP

Chronology

1869	Freedmen's Bureau discontinued
1881	Tuskegee Institute opened by Booker T. Washington
1890	Afro-American League of the United States founded to fight segregation and discrimination
1895	Booker T. Washington delivers Atlanta Exposition speech. Later referred to by W. E. B. DuBois as the "Atlanta Compromise" (September)
1895	National Association of Colored Women established with motto "Lifting As We Climb"
1896–1914	Atlanta University Conference on Negro Problems held annually to examine some phase of Afro-American life
1900	National Negro Business League organized under leadership of B. T. Washington

---

INTRODUCTORY STATEMENT

B ETWEEN 1850 AND 1900 the number of black people in the United States more than doubled, but their proportion to the total population dropped from 15.7 to 11.6 percent. The majority of Negroes lived in the South. In Mississippi and South Carolina they comprised more than 50 percent of the population; in Alabama, Florida, and Georgia, 40 percent. The end of Reconstruction brought little improvement in the economic and social status of blacks. The failure of congressional Reconstruction had reduced them to political impotency and economic peonage; segregation laws compounded their difficulties. The presence of large numbers of black people in the South helps to explain a closely drawn color line, especially in that region. The black man's struggle up from slavery was also complicated by such practices as violence against his person, calculated to terrify him into a position of subordination. All too often white candidates used "Negro-baiting," tactics that appealed to the prejudices of lower- and middle-class voters as a means of getting elected to public office. Some blacks migrated to urban areas, but the majority continued to be agricultural laborers.

Professor Franklin concludes that blacks could be certain of an improved status only in their education, for many of the schools that had been founded in the immediate postwar era were still flourishing. Negroes came to view enlightenment as the greatest single opportunity to escape the proscriptions and indignities of which they were victims. Many of their schools had been founded by religious denominations, but a new form of support emerged in the financial assistance provided by private philanthropy. Although most of the donations were made with a view to encouraging industrial education, other types of black schools did receive some assistance. By and large, white southerners showed a willingness to tolerate industrial or vocational training because blacks thereby were kept in the subordinate position of manual laborers. The availability of funds from private philanthropy had the negative effect of discouraging the equitable distribution of public funds for the education of all southern children.

The problem of education for blacks was complicated by the differing philosophies as to the best type of education. Booker T. Washington was the champion of those who felt that the Negro needed an education that would best and most rapidly equip him to find a place in the American social order. His highly publicized Atlanta Exposition speech in 1895 helped him gain acceptance by whites, fame, and power.

Washington's experiences at Hampton Institute and later at Tuskegee, which he founded, convinced him that industrial or vocational education would be particularly beneficial for his people in their present condition. Such training would not antagonize the South, would be highly acceptable to northern philanthropists, and would at the same time improve the economic position of blacks. Although not deprecating liberal arts studies, he did regard them as impractical for that time.

Despite Washington's stature, opposition to his program appeared and grew. The Afro-American League became a forum for militant protest and attacks on Washington. William Monroe Trotter, editor of the Boston *Guardian,* was an articulate critic. Prominent among Washington's opponents was William Edward Burghardt DuBois, a talented university-trained Negro. Although he shared Washington's interest in racial solidarity and self-help, he accused him of preaching a gospel of work and money exclusively, and denounced his program as one of complete accommodation. DuBois caustically referred to the Atlanta Exposition speech as the "Atlanta Compromise," claiming that Washington had practically conceded the alleged inferiority of black people.

The struggle of black people for economic security was hindered by the unwillingness of the stronger labor unions to accept them as members. Frustrated in their attempt to participate in white business enterprises, blacks embarked on a program of "Negro business enterprise" with some success in certain areas. Socially and culturally, Negroes maintained a separate existence. Important agencies for maintaining group cohesion were black churches, fraternal orders, and mutual benefit associations, which fostered the emergence of a substantial number of talented Afro-Americans who were both creative and articulate.

STUDY NOTES

Pages 268–272, *Education and philanthropy*. Despite some opposition, southerners seemed more willing to tolerate black educational institutions than any other self-help agencies of Afro-Americans. The growth of schools in the postwar period coincided with the emergence of a new form of financial support—northern philanthropy. For private church-sponsored institutions, this was a welcome supplement to denominational support; furthermore, the philanthropists had more money at their disposal than did the churches. Note the listing and descriptions of foundations that worked to advance, or contributed to the advance of Negro education. Whatever their motives—and they were not always unselfish—these funds stimulated a broadening of educational concepts for black people in the South. On the other hand, philanthropic support had a negative effect in that it quite probably provided one excuse for the inequitable distribution of tax money for the education of all southern children. Whites could rationalize that if philanthropists were going to educate blacks, tax money could be used to educate whites. In any event, disproportionate amounts of public funds were expended for the training of white children. State and local officials could comfort themselves with their contention that, since blacks paid little in taxes, their schools and teachers were not entitled to much financial assistance from public monies. This contention was opposed, with little success, by blacks.

Pages 274–277, *Booker T. Washington and his program*. Born in slavery at Hales Ford, Virginia, graduate of Hampton Institute, and founder of Tuskegee Institute, Booker T. Washington's ascent to fame and power was remarkable. From his experiences at Hampton and Tuskegee evolved a program of black-betterment which included such postulates as accommodation, ownership of land, habits of thrift, self-help, and the cultivation of high morals and good manners. This program was grounded on the contemporary moral-economic ideology and on a philosophy of cooperation with southern whites. As you read the material in these pages, you will notice that the author cites both the strong and weak points in this program. Bear in mind that from today's vantage point, the weaknesses—which were indisputably present—are more apparent than they were to Washington's generation.

Pages 277–280, *Opposition of W. E. B. DuBois*. As might be expected, Washington's program and philosophy met with opposition from some blacks, for various reasons. The foremost critic of the Tuskegeean was Dr. W. E. B. DuBois. He opposed Washington's narrow educational objectives and his acceptance of the black man's subordinate political and civil status. He contended that it was not possible, under modern competitive methods, for black artisans, businessmen, and property owners to exist and defend their rights without the vote. If you should read them, you would find both DuBois' *Souls of Black Folk* and Washington's autobiography *Up From Slavery* interesting and revealing.

Pages 280–287, *Struggles in the economic sphere*. The efforts of blacks to earn a living and to accumulate a land or money base were complicated by a number of factors. Most blacks were without capital with which to buy land; thus they often worked simply as agricultural laborers under some form of tenancy or sharecropping. Those who had the money found it difficult to purchase arable land, while those who owned land knew little, if anything about modern methods of crop production. These unfavorable conditions prompted a number of blacks to migrate to other sections that they regarded as more attractive. Blacks themselves were in disagreement as to the wisdom of leaving the South. Industrial opportunities in the South failed to benefit blacks to any great extent, although black inventors contributed measurably to the industrial growth of the North. A color line within the ranks of organized labor effectively barred the black worker. Only the Knights of Labor, which welcomed into its ranks both skilled and unskilled, white and black workers, had a fairly large number of black members. This organization eventually disintegrated, and the more permanent American Federation of Labor found ways of excluding the Negro laborer. Blacks attempted to establish their own separate unions, but their organizations were at best weak and temporary. More success attended their separate business enterprises, and in the field of banking a tenuous foothold was established.

Pages 287–291, *Social and cultural growth.* Finding themselves cut off from the mainstream of life in America, black people were forced to maintain a separate social and cultural existence. Their independent social institutions helped them sustain a viable, cohesive group life. As it had done in the past, the church played a significant role. The black church was as disturbed by the forces let loose by the "gilded age" in America as was the white church. Social Darwinism had the effect of compelling religious leaders to question orthodox religion, and brought to the fore a conflict between conservative, or orthodox, elements on the one hand and modernist, or progressive, groups on the other. Out of this conflict came a growing trend toward the "socialization" of church functions. Many blacks turned also to their fraternal orders and benefit associations for social outlet, as well as for protection against the exigencies of life. Conventions and conferences also served as avenues for expressing black concerns.

Pages 291–294, *A black vanguard.* There emerged a group of intellectually mature and talented blacks who expressed themselves through various media. Newspapers, especially those published weekly, had wide readership and helped disseminate the concerns and news of blacks. The black man's experiences up to this point demonstrated that he would have to be responsible for his own development within the American "melting pot."

SELF-TEST

Multiple Choice

1. The end of Reconstruction:
   a. had the effect of insuring the ballot to blacks.
   b. brought little improvement in the economic and social status of black people.
   c. coincided with the unwillingness of whites to tolerate separate black schools in their midst.
   d. decreased racial antagonism.

2. Which of these established a fund that provided substantial financial assistance for the education of Negroes in the South?
    a. John F. Slater.
    b. George Peabody.
    c. Anna T. Jeanes.
    d. all three.

3. Which of these men advised his people to "cast down your bucket where you are"?
    a. T. Thomas Fortune.
    b. W. E. B. DuBois.
    c. Booker T. Washington.
    d. Richard T. Greener.

4. Booker T. Washington and W. E. B. DuBois:
    a. shared identical philosophies of Negro betterment.
    b. both showed relative disinterest in political and civil rights for blacks.
    c. were in agreement as to the type of education for black people.
    d. both advocated programs of Negro betterment.

5. One basic reason why Negroes in large numbers did not become a permanent part of the organized labor movement was that:
    a. most were too lazy to work.
    b. since the majority of black workers were skilled, they could make more money outside the unions.
    c. most white workers were prejudiced against black workers.
    d. black laborers voluntarily remained aloof.

Fill in the Blanks

1. _____ The author refers to him as "the central figure—the dominant personality—in the history of the Negro down to his death in 1915."

2. _____ This leader opposed the exodus of blacks from the South on the grounds that the government should protect citizens wherever they live.

3. _____ This national labor union, which placed little emphasis on skills, was the only one that made black workers welcome as members.

4. _____ He was the author of the "first historical study by a Negro to be taken seriously by American scholars."

5. _____ Author of numerous works, his *The Suppression of the African Slave Trade* is the first scientific historical monograph written by a black man.

True or False

_____1. Philanthropists contributed substantially to the improvement of education for Negroes in the South.

_____2. Philanthropists did much to encourage the equitable distribution of tax money for educating all southern children.

_____3. The doctrine of vocational education for the black masses met with the general disapproval of most whites.

_____4. There were valid objections to Washington's program for the salvation of black people.

_____5. All black leaders agreed that it was desirable for Negroes to leave the South and seek work elsewhere.

Essay Questions

1. Analyze Washington's program for Negro betterment. What, in your opinion, were its strengths? its weaknesses?
2. On what grounds did DuBois criticize or oppose the program set forth by Washington? Evaluate the validity of DuBois' criticisms.
3. Compare and contrast church philanthropy with that of the large private foundations.
4. a. What problems made it difficult for blacks to adjust economically as farmers in the postwar South?
   b. Describe the relationship of black workers to organized labor in the postwar period.
5. Cite evidences of the black man's intellectual growth around the turn of the century in the United States.

Identify and/or Define

philanthropy
noblesse oblige
deprecate
monograph
peonage

Moses "Pap"
   Singleton
Henry Adams
Richard T. Greener
T. Thomas Fortune

Madam C. J. Walker
Henry Ossian Flipper
George Washington
   Williams

chapter XVII

ENLARGED DIMENSIONS OF RACIAL CONFLICT

Chronology

1898	Spanish-American War
1901	President Theodore Roosevelt dines with B. T. Washington at the White House
1905–1908	Niagara Movement committed to securing full and complete citizenship for black people
1906	Brownsville, Texas, racial disturbance for which black soldiers were blamed and subsequently dishonorably discharged (August)
1906	Atlanta race riot, the South's most sensational (September)
1908	Springfield, Illinois, race riot, led to founding of the National Association for the Advancement of Colored People
1909	National Association for the Advancement of Colored People founded to fight for full civil rights primarily through legal action
1911	National Urban League created through merger of three existing organizations to widen economic opportunities and help black migrants in adjusting to urban problems

INTRODUCTORY STATEMENT

FOLLOWING THE Civil War, the United States was preoccupied with domestic problems and activities, which in large measure resulted from the tremendous industrial thrust generated by the war. There was a growing interest in territorial acquisition and in the possibility of the resulting expanded economic and political influence. The United States observed with continuing interest an expansion of European power in Africa and Asia. Before the outbreak of war with Spain, the nation's leaders demonstrated a commitment to the acquisition of noncontiguous territory through the purchase of Alaska from Russia, and showed a keen interest in Samoa. At about the same time, but not as a result of the Spanish-American War, Hawaii was annexed. Meanwhile, jurisdiction was extended over other areas, primarily in the Pacific where the inhabitants were for the most part "darker peoples." The Spanish-American War itself is a dramatic illustration of the new mood of "manifest destiny," or imperialism, that was to be seen in late nineteenth-century America.

Black Americans were as much opposed to Spain's dictatorial rule in Cuba as were white Americans. They were affected by the lurid and some-times misrepresented exposés by the "yellow press" of Spanish ill-treatment of Cubans, and they shared in the indignation of the entire coun-try when the battleship *Maine* was sunk in the Havana harbor. Anxious to help bring independence to Cuba, Afro-Americans offered their services as volunteers when war broke out between the United States and Spain in 1898. The only blacks who saw considerable service in this war were the members of the four Negro units in the regular army. Those who saw action in this short war participated in most of the heavy fighting and per-formed gallantly in the famous charge up San Juan Hill. It should be noted that black sailors also lost their lives in this conflict, though they had few opportunities to demonstrate fighting ability.

Despite an increase in the number of social, economic, and political problems that plagued a rapidly industrializing nation, the turn of the cen-tury was a time of hope for most Americans. People's thinking embraced a host of optimistic ideas which can best be bundled together and labeled "progressivism." While Progressives recognized all sorts of faults and shortcomings in American society, they believed that these could be reme-died by reform. Yet, symptomatic of the thought of the day on racial mat-ters, most Progressives overlooked the problems associated with being black in the United States. Few Negroes participated in the Progressive movement and most wings of progressivism deliberately excluded blacks. Ironically, during this period of reform, the position of blacks in American society worsened, with the lines of segregation more tightly drawn.

A familiar pattern of violence became more pronounced as the rate of lynchings increased and an epidemic of race riots spread. Although some of the more sensational riots occurred in the South, they were not confined to that region. The northern riot that stimulated organized reaction from blacks and concerned whites was the one that took place in Springfield, Illinois, in August 1908. Earlier, in 1905, W. E. B. DuBois and a group of young, talented, and militant blacks had launched a counterattack in the now-famous Niagara Movement. This group met under DuBois' leadership at Niagara Falls and made plans for a more effective attack on discrimina-tion. Several subsequent annual meetings were held at historic "freedom" spots, but positive accomplishments were disappointing to its members. Nevertheless, the Niagara Movement was significant in that it contributed to other black protest movements, particularly to the formation of the National Association for the Advancement of Colored People (NAACP).

The Springfield riot was the immediate stimulus for the formation of a permanent organization pledged to work for the attainment of first-class citizenship for Afro-Americans. Formally organized in May 1910 as the National Association for the Advancement of Colored People, its member-ship was interracial, with DuBois as its only Negro national officer ini-tially. Well organized and operating through branches, the NAACP set in motion a forward-looking program designed to eliminate discrimination in the United States. Its most dramatic successes came through legal action, beginning in 1915.

The plight of the black migrant in the city received the sympathetic attention of the National Urban League, whose organization was perfected in 1911. This organization worked to open new opportunities for blacks in industry and assisted migrants in their problems of adjustment in urban centers.

The work of these two groups, supplemented by the efforts of other agencies, offered positive solutions for old problems. But the plight of black people in the new century was too deep-rooted and complex for easy solution in an atmosphere so charged with prejudice.

STUDY NOTES

Pages 295–297, *The extension of American influence.* After the Civil War, the United States sought and found investment markets and sources of raw materials in areas outside its continental boundaries. Most of these were in the Caribbean or the Pacific and were populated largely by nonwhite peoples. Among the early acquisitions were Alaska, Hawaii, Tutuila in the Samoan islands, and other small Pacific islands. Where territory was not annexed outright, American control was assured through the extension of financial interests and increasing political influence, backed by the presence of United States Marines as, for example, in the Dominican Republic.

Pages 297–298, *The Spanish-American War.* For various reasons, not the least of which was the influence of certain "yellow journals" in stimulating a jingoistic spirit among Americans, the United States went to war against Spain. Basic to the war aim was a determination that Cubans be set free from Spanish control and given their independence. You should note that this war aim was not honored in reality.

Pages 298–302, *Blacks in the Spanish-American War.* As before, black Americans volunteered their services in this war. However, most black soldiers who saw combat service were members of the four black units in the regular army. Others who saw duty were those in specially created units or in outfits of a number of states. Those who fought, the "Smoked Yankees," performed with gallantry. However, later comments by Theodore Roosevelt relative to the performance of black troops varied from unqualified praise to criticism, depending upon the occasion. Black Americans were to learn that as President, the "Rough Rider's" reactions were neither consistent nor predictable where they were concerned.

Page 302, *Civilian hostility to the black soldier.* On a number of occasions, southern whites gave vent to their disapproval of the arming of blacks as servicemen. Troops either passing through or stationed in the South were the recipients of contemptuous actions and words.

Pages 303–308, *America's Negro empire.* At the end of the Spanish-American War the United States could regard itself as an imperialistic power. The treaty with Spain provided for the independence of Cuba (which in reality became an American protectorate), and for the cession of Puerto Rico, Guam, and the Philippines to the United States. These regions possessed natural resources and were potential markets for American products. They were uniformly populated by so-called "backward peoples," and in most cases they were darker peoples. This immediately presented one of the more troublesome of the American imperial difficulties because it was related to the domestic color "problem." The United

States felt it necessary to pursue an imperial policy with regard to race that would upset the racial equilibrium at home.

Pages 308–310, *The promise of the twentieth century.* Despite an increase in social, economic, and political problems which characterized a highly industrialized America at the beginning of the twentieth century, Afro-Americans were optimistic concerning their future. They viewed with favor the succession to the presidency of Theodore Roosevelt, and were pleased with some of his early actions with regard to black people. Note, for example, his having lunch with Booker T. Washington at the White House and his apparent lack of concern over outraged southern reaction. Washington and Roosevelt enjoyed a close relationship, but unfortunately, their friendship did little, if anything, to improve racial relations with any degree of significance.

Pages 310–313, *Urban problems.* The century that had opened on a high note of optimism soon presented new problems for black Americans that were as difficult to cope with as earlier ones. Difficulties of adjustment faced by all unskilled migrants to urban areas were often magnified for the black newcomer. Continued immigration from rural areas aggravated the key problems of finding decent jobs and housing. Adding to their woes was the pattern of residential segregation, which had the effect of crowding them into one section of the city, a pattern stamped with the approval of some of the municipalities themselves. Undesirable results could be detected in widespread disorganization and disintegration of families, often accompanied by a rise in the incidence of juvenile delinquency.

Pages 313–318, *The pattern of violence.* Black people soon understood that the optimistic promise of the new century was to be unfulfilled. For them, the new era meant more violence and bloodshed in the forms of lynchings and race riots. Not content with the systematic movement already underway to disfranchise the black man and to degrade him socially, white bigots poured out their wrath on black people in the North and the South. As you note in these pages the localities and features of racial disturbances, you will understand that the pattern followed was about the same everywhere.

Page 318, *The Niagara Movement.* The plight of Afro-Americans in this century prompted a group of young, talented, and militant Negroes to organize and demand that all racial discrimination be ended. They wanted nothing less than a complete elimination of all distinctions based on race. Under the leadership of W. E. B. DuBois, this group held its organizational meeting at Niagara Falls, Canada, in June 1905. Note in the text the platform of the Niagara Movement, and read the excerpt from its manifesto. Subsequent annual meetings were held, but positive accomplishments were disappointing to its members, and the Movement was absorbed by a more permanent organization.

Pages 318–320, *Founding of the NAACP.* One result of the Springfield, Illinois, race riot was the issuance of a call by a group of distinguished Americans for a conference to be held on the centennial of Lincoln's birthday. Out of this first meeting in 1909 came a formal organization which was perfected in May 1910. This was the National Association for the Advancement of Colored People. It launched a crusade to curb lynching and lawlessness, to secure the franchise for blacks, and to end all forms of segregation and discrimination. Early in its existence it established a pattern of seeking court action to secure its objectives. The literary organ of the NAACP was the *Crisis,* of which DuBois was first editor.

Page 321, *The National Urban League.* One of the more important, enduring, and effective of the national organizations designed to assist black people in their struggle for equal rights is the National League on Urban Conditions among Negroes, better known by the shorter title, the National Urban League. Its chief focus was on the improvement of the quality of life for black men and women in cities.

SELF-TEST

Multiple Choice

1. Term applied to black soldiers by Spaniards in the Spanish-American War:
   a. "Black Thunderbolts."
   b. "Smoked Yankees."
   c. "Muckrakers."
   d. "Butchers."

2. United States imperialism included annexing all of the following *except:*
   a. Hawaii.
   b. Formosa.
   c. the Philippines.
   d. Puerto Rico.

3. As late as 1900, the United States:
   a. had eliminated segregation in all public schools.
   b. was a nation in which all citizens enjoyed the equal protection of the law.
   c. was still primarily a racist nation.
   d. had acted vigorously to prevent disfranchisement of blacks.

4. As President, Theodore Roosevelt pleased Negroes when he:
   a. dined with Booker T. Washington at the White House.
   b. appointed a black man to the collectorship of the port of Charleston, South Carolina.
   c. refused to accept the forced resignation of the Negro postmistress at Indianola, Mississippi.
   d. did all of the above.

5. Which one is not true of the "muckrakers"? They:
   a. attacked wretched slum conditions.
   b. exposed corruption in city government.
   c. assailed the privileged position of huge business corporations.
   d. espoused a formal program for the securing of civil rights for black men and women.

Fill in the Blanks

the Marine

1. _____ The sinking of this United States battleship in the Havana harbor helped bring on the Spanish-American War.

Charles Young

2. _____ This West Pointer was the only black commissioned officer in the country at the outbreak of the Spanish-American War.

Muckerackers

3. _____ Derogatory term applied by Roosevelt to those writers who attacked the ills of early twentieth-century American society.

W E B DuBois

4. _____ Leader of the Niagara Movement and first editor of the *Crisis*.

National urban League

5. _____ Agency successful in widening opportunities for blacks in industrial employment and in helping black people to solve problems peculiar to the cities.

True or False

___ 1. Black Americans were particularly disturbed by the succession to the presidency of Theodore Roosevelt.

___ 2. Some municipalities gave official sanction to the practice of residential segregation.

___ 3. Coincident with the rise of the American city was the rise of the black community within the city.

___ 4. It was in Africa that the United States pursued its new imperialistic policy most vigorously.

___ 5. At the outbreak of the Spanish-American War there were no Negro units in the regular army.

Essay Questions

1. Name three noncontiguous territories acquired by the United States between 1898 and 1917. Show how the "problem" of color at home affected United States imperial policy.
2. a. By what various means did black men get into the Spanish-American War?
   b. Comment briefly on their actions as soldiers in this war.
3. Discuss the plight of Afro-Americans in an urban, industrial society in the early years of the twentieth century.

4. Identify and describe two or three programs and responses that evolved as a result of attempts to solve problems facing black Americans. Evaluate the degree of success these programs had.
5. What early actions of President Roosevelt persuaded Negroes that he was their friend? Did his handling of the Brownsville affair justify this feeling?

Identify and/or Define

imperialism
contiguous
sovereignty
jingoistic
protectorate
"yellow journalism"
cavalry

"muckrakers"
dollar diplomacy
Ray Stannard Baker
Valeriano Weyler
Rough Riders
"Black Thunderbolt"

"Smoked Yankees"
"Square Deal"
Niagara Movement
NAACP
National Urban
  League

chapter XVIII

IN PURSUIT OF DEMOCRACY

Chronology

1915 Blatantly antiblack motion picture *Birth of a Nation* released
1916 Amenia (N.Y.) Conference called to plot strategy for continued attack on all distinctions based on race
1917 United States enters World War I (April)
1917 At Fort Des Moines, Iowa, 639 black candidates become commissioned officers in U.S. Army (October)
1918 DuBois "Close Ranks" editorial in the *Crisis* gives support to the war effort
1919 Pan-African Congress, called by DuBois in Paris

INTRODUCTORY STATEMENT

T O THE AMERICAN people, preoccupied with their own domestic problems, World War I came as a shock. Signs of war had long been evident in a Europe characterized by militarism, imperialism, and nationalism. In a futile attempt to maintain peace, rival coalitions of nations had been established, but the balance of power was upset in 1914. At the outset of war, black people were not concerned with foreign problems. Their interest was focused on newly elected President Woodrow Wilson and prospects held out for them in his "New Freedom" program. Their hopes for improvement faded, however, in the face of anti-Negro legislation proposed by the first Congress of Wilson's administration and of officially sanctioned segregation in the District of Columbia.

Despite their disappointment, black men were among those who thronged to the recruiting stations when the United States declared war on Germany in April 1917. For the most part, these volunteers were rejected. The Selective Service Act, however, provided for the enlistment of all able-bodied men between the ages of 21 and 31. In spite of a seeming eagerness to draft blacks, southerners were generally opposed to having draftees, especially northern blacks, trained in their communities.

After the completion of basic training, most black soldiers were assigned to labor battalions and service units. Pressure from Negroes led finally to the establishment of an officers' training camp for officer candidates.

In the face of ever-present evidence of distasteful discrimination at home and overseas, black troops served their country well. Two black combat divisions, the Ninety-Second and Ninety-Third, faced their own peculiar difficulties. Black soldiers did their job well even though subjected to such dampers on morale as contemptuous treatment by their fellow white American counterparts and officers, as well as German propaganda designed to capitalize on the situation. Feats of gallantry performed by Afro-Americans were similar to those of other American fighting men. These feats received high praise, and in a number of instances, led to citations for bravery under fire.

Negroes on the home front gave their full support to the war effort. Plagued by worsening race relations, black people contributed both their money and labor to the cause of victory. Perhaps they reasoned that this would provide additional grounds for their demands for equal treatment when the war ended. On the whole, they supported the call of DuBois to "close ranks" and fight alongside white citizens in the war effort. Economic and social considerations led hundreds of blacks to migrate out of the South during the war years. Even though they encountered hostility and unfortunate antiblack incidents in the North and West, they also found greater opportunities in industrial employment and more justice in the courts.

STUDY NOTES

Pages 323–325, *Afro-Americans at the outbreak of World War I.* At the outbreak of the First World War, black Americans were too concerned with pressing problems at home to evidence interest in European affairs. Their hopes for a better day faded when, as President, Woodrow Wilson demonstrated a lack of commitment to improving their lot. It was Wilson who gave presidential sanction to the segregation of the races in the federal departments in Washington, D.C. They were further disenchanted by his treatment of a committee of blacks led by Monroe Trotter, who had gained an audience with the President to protest segregation. An increase in the number of lynchings and the mob violence that followed the release of the antiblack motion picture *Birth of a Nation* added to their distress. The death of Booker T. Washington in 1915 left no spokesman or leader for the race, but the next year at the Amenia Conference, a distinguished group pledged themselves to work for racial betterment.

Pages 325–331, *The enlistment of blacks.* When the United States entered the war, black men met stern resistance in their efforts to gain commissions in the Army. Barred from the marines and permitted to serve in the navy only in menial capacities, black men served in almost every branch of the army. The training of Negro soldiers was, at best, irregular. The units of one black division were trained in separate camps and were never put together as a division until they were overseas. Both trainees and those who completed basic training faced constant discrimination. The difficulties were compounded by the hostility of southern whites to the Negro presence in their communities. Friction between Negro soldiers and military police, clashes between black and white soldiers, and constant harassment by civilians were frequent. Disheartening incidents involving white citizens occurred in such places as Spartanburg, South Carolina, and Houston, Texas.

Pages 331–338, *Black servicemen overseas.* Even though the first black servicemen to arrive in Europe were members of service outfits, a large number saw active combat duty. On the whole, their service was commendable, and in a number of instances went beyond the call of duty. Factors such as the condescending attitude of some white commanding officers, along with the attempt to persuade the French people that black soldiers were depraved and a potential social danger did nothing to boost their morale. In spite of this, black soldiers performed as gallantly as did other soldiers. Individual acts of bravery were cited by both the American and French governments. In an effort to maintain high morale, most combat units had their own bands. This was important to men whose units were invariably bypassed by organized white entertainment groups. Welfare work was carried on by such organizations as the YMCA and YWCA. Helping to build morale was the friendly spirit of the French people and the respect that they gave the black soldiers. Note that the British military attitude was also favorable to black troops.

Pages 338–343, *The home front.* Black Americans at home supported the successful prosecution of the war. An important social and economic phenomenon of the times was the migration of large numbers of Negroes out of the South. Even though the North and West did not turn out to be the "promised land," hundreds of blacks preferred to take their chances in new surroundings. Organized labor continued to exclude black workers from its membership rolls. Also on the negative side was the sordid record of lynching and race clashes that continued to darken race relations in the nation. The author notes that while there was a vigorous pursuit of democracy in Europe there was widespread destruction of democracy at home. Afro-Americans learned that for them, democracy in the United States was to continue to be both elusive and ephemeral. The prediction that the problem of the twentieth century was to be "the problem of the color line" was indeed being fulfilled.

SELF-TEST

Multiple Choice

1. As President, Woodrow Wilson by executive order:
   a. segregated black federal employees in eating and rest room facilities.
   b. phased out most blacks from civil service.
   c. did both of the above.
   d. did neither of the above.

2. Large numbers of southern Negroes migrated to the North during World War I because of:
   a. increased southern repression.
   b. economic opportunities resulting from the war.

c. a feeling that the North was the land of promise.
d. all of the above.

3. The movie *Birth of a Nation:*
   a. glorified black manhood.
   b. told a positive and accurate story of black emancipation.
   c. was blatantly anti-Negro.
   d. received little, if any, attention from the public.

4. In World War I blacks were barred altogether from the:
   a. cavalry.
   b. marines.
   c. engineer corps.
   d. stevedore regiments.

5. During the First World War, white southerners:
   a. welcomed the stationing of northern black soldiers in their communities.
   b. supported the move to grant blacks army commissions.
   c. advocated the creation of integrated military units.
   d. objected strenuously to the army's sending northern blacks into the South for training.

Fill in the Blanks

1. _Ninety-Second_ The irregular procedure of training separate units of this black division was followed during World War I.

2. _369th U.S. Infantry_ Called "Hell Fighters" by the Germans, this regiment's bravery under fire earned for it the French *Croix de Guerre.*

3. _Emmett J. Scott_ Appointed special assistant to the Secretary of War, he served as confidential advisor in matters relating to Negroes.

4. _the Messenger_ Black newspaper, published in New York by A. Philip Randolph and Chandler Owen, that refused to give all-out support to the war.

5. _Battle of Henry Johnson_ This term given to the sensational feat of a black private in helping to repulse a German raiding party in May 1918.

True or False

_T_ 1. The Ninety-Second Division was the only one that did not train together as a unit.

_F_ 2. The lack of friction between white southerners and black soldiers was pleasing to the War Department.

_F_ 3. The first black servicemen to arrive in Europe were combat troops.

_T_ 4. Units of the Ninety-Third Division were scattered among various divisions of the French army.

_T_ 5. The black press, for the most part, supported the war enthusiastically.

Essay Questions

1. How did the Selective Service Act of May 18, 1917, affect the enlistment of blacks? Although the act itself was not discriminatory, in some cases its implementation was. Explain.
2. Comment on the peculiar problems encountered by black draftees. How did the War Department react to these problems?
3. a. How do you account for the increased migration of blacks from the South during World War I?
   b. What were some results of this exodus?
4. Describe the activities of the 369th United States Infantry as a combat unit.
5. How did the reaction of the black press to World War I reflect the feelings of W. E. B. DuBois toward the war effort? What significance can you see in the generally supportive attitude by the black press? Do you detect an ulterior motive?

Identify and/or Define

blatant
canteen
mandate
exodus
stevedore
Colonel Charles
   Young

Joel Spingarn
Emmett J. Scott
Robert R. Moton
The *Messenger*
Pan-African

League of Nations
Associated Colored
   Employees of
   America

chapter XIX

DEMOCRACY ESCAPES

Chronology

1915   Ku Klux Klan revived; becomes a militant white-supremacist social and political force in 1920s

1916   Marcus Garvey organizes a New York chapter of the black nationalist Universal Negro Improvement Association

1919   The "Red Summer" witnessed an epidemic of race riots all over the United States

1925   Brotherhood of Sleeping Car Porters and Maids organized by A. Philip Randolph

---

INTRODUCTORY STATEMENT

U PON THEIR RETURN from Europe after World War I, black soldiers found themselves thrust into an atmosphere of racial antipathy and hostility. The enthusiastic reception accorded the first returnees was confined to New York, it seemed, and was of short duration. Mob violence, spearheaded by a revived Ku Klux Klan, reflected the determination of bigoted whites—North, South, and West—to keep black people in a condition of second-class citizenship.

The "Red Summer" of 1919 witnessed the greatest period of interracial strife the nation had ever seen up to that time. Race riots became a fact of life for many urban blacks. The apparent willingness of the Negro to die in his own defense injected a new equation into the postwar racial strife. Under such depressed conditions, the NAACP launched an unsuccessful campaign to secure passage of a federal antilynching law. Other groups emerged, but they were rarely able to accomplish more than the passing of resolutions of protest. These were generally interracial groups to which middle-class blacks and liberal whites belonged.

The man who captured the imagination and loyalty of thousands of black men and women was Marcus Garvey. The program of this "Black Moses" attracted a wide following from those on whom the stress and strain of a hostile urban environment lay heaviest. The basis of his popularity was his appeal to race pride and the exaltation of everything black. He insisted that black stood for strength and beauty rather than inferiority, and he asserted that Africans had a noble past of which Afro-Americans should be proud. Feeling that there was no hope in America, he counseled Negroes to return to Africa. This is characterized as the first real mass movement among blacks in the history of the United States, and it mirrored the disillusionment of millions of black Americans.

The "prosperity" of the 1920s was not shared by many black people. Thus, it was no surprise that when depression came to the United States, blacks were among those hardest hit. Even when organized programs of relief were put into operation, Negroes were the victims of discrimination because assistance was seldom administered on an equal basis.

STUDY NOTES

Pages 344–349, *Postwar reaction*. Returning black veterans who paraded up Fifth Avenue in New York City during the victory celebrations were hopeful of enjoying at home the same principles of equality they had observed abroad. Those returning black troops who received a warm welcome were pleased with their reception. The period of jubilation was short-lived, however, for soon an unfortunate reaction set in. Taking their cue from a revived Ku Klux Klan, bigoted whites across the nation began a widespread campaign of violence and intimidation aimed at keeping black people "in their places." The summer of 1919 has been aptly designated "The Red Summer," for it ushered in "the greatest period of racial strife the nation had ever witnessed." The most serious riot took place in Chicago. Study the analysis in the textbook of the underlying causes of racial animosity in a crowded urban area.

Pages 350–351, *The Negro counterreaction*. Urbanization was accompanied by a stimulation of self-respect and black cohesiveness. To many whites, a readiness on the part of black people to stand up and defend themselves came from foreign influences. This view was ridiculed by black leaders who pointed out that they were battling only for what they thought was right.

Pages 351–354, *The voice of protest arises*. In the postwar years Negroes continued to use the meetings of their national organizations as forums from which they could register their protest against the failure of the United States to grant them equal citizenship. The best known and most permanent of the groups was the NAACP. Unable to get its anti-lynching bill through Congress, it had greater success in the attempt to get the all-white Democratic primaries abolished by the Supreme Court. These legal victories benefited those blacks who participated in the political process at the state and local levels, but such middle-class, biracial organizations as the NAACP failed to attract the black masses.

Pages 354–356, *Marcus Garvey, the "Black Moses."* A feeling that older and better-established bodies were not joining hands with them in their efforts to better themselves helps explain why the masses of black people were attracted to Marcus Garvey and his Universal Negro Improvement Association. Appealing to race pride, exalting blackness, and holding out the prospect of returning to the African homeland, Garvey provided a possibility of escape for thousands of blacks trapped in what had become urban ghettos. Operating through a number of auxiliary units, he enlisted thousands of blacks who regarded themselves as citizens of an entirely new empire. Displaying their own flag, whose colors were black, green, and red, his followers paraded in colorful uniforms and held conferences and conventions. Although hailed by many as a true "Black Moses," the established black leadership denounced him as an "insincere, selfish impostor." Garvey, in turn, castigated them as opportunistic integrationists who were traitors to their race. His most caustic comments were reserved for DuBois and other NAACP leaders. Alleged irregularities in the conduct of his Black Star Line led to his imprisonment and eventual deportation as an undesirable alien. More than any before him, Garvey dramatized the frustrations and alienation of the black masses.

Pages 357–360, *Depression and the Negro.* Although the number of potential black wage earners expanded in the 1920s, many others joined the ranks of the unemployed. Labor unions continued their policy of Negro exclusion. This state of affairs caused a number of blacks to form the "Friends of Negro Freedom." Its work was largely ineffective, as was the work of similar groups. The "most significant step toward the unionization of Negroes" was the creation of the Brotherhood of Sleeping Car Porters and Maids by A. Philip Randolph in 1925. Full recognition finally came to this union in 1937 when the Pullman Company recognized it as the bargaining agency for the porters and maids employed by the company. Most black businesses were limited in their income capacity by the fact that their clients were most often Negroes, whose incomes and employment were often uncertain. Agrarian distress in the South played havoc with all farmers, and the number of black farm owners decreased. After the coming of the Great Depression, many more workers found themselves unemployed and on the relief rolls. The specter of starvation forced large numbers of blacks to apply for relief, but often they were discriminated against in the administration of welfare dollars and food supplies.

SELF-TEST

Multiple Choice

1. Which of the following most accurately describes the Ku Klux Klan of the postwar years?
   a. Unlike the first Klan, it welcomed black members.
   b. It was a racist, reactionary white supremacist organization.
   c. Its membership was confined to the South.
   d. It condemned violence as a means of achieving its objectives.

2. This black leader exalted blackness and urged his people to return to Africa:
   a. A. Philip Randolph.
   b. James Weldon Johnson.
   c. Marcus Garvey.
   d. Walter White.

3. An epidemic of race riots, beginning in the summer of this year, led to its designation as the "Red Summer":
   a. 1919.

b. 1920.

c. 1929.

d. 1930.

4. In the case of *Smith* v. *Allwright,* the U.S. Supreme Court held that:
   a. the grandfather clause violated the Constitution.
   b. residential segregation ordinances were unconstitutional.
   c. each state must provide integrated educational opportunities for all its citizens.
   d. the exclusion of blacks from the Democratic primary was a violation of the Fifteenth Amendment.

5. The "most significant step" toward black unionization taken in the 1920s was the formation of the:
   a. National Association for the Promotion of Labor Unionism among Negroes.
   b. Friends of Negro Freedom.
   c. Brotherhood of Sleeping Car Porters and Maids.
   d. American Negro Labor Congress.

Fill in the Blanks

1. _____ Term applied to the summer of 1919 because of the intensity and widespread nature of racial strife then.

2. _____ Leader, called by some the "Black Moses," who stressed racial pride and exalted blackness.

3. _____ Name of the black nationalist organization founded by the "Black Moses."

4. _____ Most successful black union of the postwar period, founded by A. Philip Randolph.

5. _____ Racist, reactionary white supremacist organization that was revived in 1915 and flourished in the United States in the 1920s.

True or False

_____ 1. Most black soldiers who served in France refused to return to the United States after the war.

_____ 2. Hindering the work of the NAACP was its policy of excluding whites from membership.

_____ 3. The most serious racial outbreak of the summer of 1919 occurred in Chicago.

_____4. None of the black organizations sensed the need for a federal antilynching law.

_____5. In the first signs of recession in the mid-1920s, large numbers of blacks lost their jobs.

Essay Questions

1. Argue for or against the proposition that the Ku Klux Klan was primarily responsible for the violent and terroristic actions against black people in the postwar period.
2. How do you account for the emergence and rise of Marcus Garvey? Be as specific as possible. What was the significance of his rise?
3. Comment on the Texas primary cases involving the right of black citizens to vote in primary elections of the Democratic party. On what grounds did the Supreme Court justify its decision in the case of *Grovey* v. *Townsend*?
4. Comment briefly on and give the significance of each of the following:
   a. Representative L. C. Dyer
   b. Walter White
   c. A. Philip Randolph
   d. George Baker

Identify and/or Define

malodorous
filibuster
peon
impostor
amalgamation
approbation

alien
"Red Summer"
"Negro Zionism"
"Black Moses"
The *Negro World*
The *Southern Frontier*

white primary
The Commission on
    Interracial
    Cooperation
Friends of Negro
    Freedom

chapter XX

THE HARLEM RENAISSANCE

Chronology

1921   *Shuffle Along*, black musical revue written and produced by blacks opened in New York

1922   Publication of Claude McKay's *Harlem Shadows*. McKay regarded as first significant writer of the Harlem Renaissance

1924   Paul Robeson played leading role in *All God's Chillun Got Wings*. Marked first time in American history that a black man had taken a principal role opposite a white woman

1925   Appearance of *Color*, Countee Cullen's first volume of poems marked a new high in the Harlem Renaissance

1929   *Hallelujah*, the first major all-black motion picture is released

1939   Daughters of the American Revolution refused to permit Marian Anderson to sing in Constitution Hall

1940   Richard Wright's *Native Son* published. Won both critical and popular acclaim

1952   Ralph Ellison's *The Invisible Man* received the National Book Award

INTRODUCTORY STATEMENT

I N THE POST-WORLD WAR I period a small contingent of writers directed attention to the faults and inadequacies of capitalistic democracy in the United States. These shortcomings weighed most heavily on America's black people. During this same time their restlessness was articulated in literature, music, and art. Although this black renaissance was part of the general trend in American literary circles, certain developments made it distinctive. Obvious discrepancies between the American promise of freedom and their actual experiences left black men and women bitter and impatient. This keen realization of injustice, along with an improvement of the capacity for expression, combined to produce a crop of black writers who constituted the "Harlem (or Black) Renaissance." During this period of literary rebirth, black writers, poets, actors, artists, and musicians won significant recognition for their creativity and talents. These individuals produced works that were generally racial in theme, but not confined to race in either content or appeal.

In the twenties, Harlem, in New York City, was the largest and most cosmopolitan Negro urban community in the United States. It had become the center of intellectual and cultural life of black America. It was only natural that the Black Renaissance should have developed there. Talented authors, playwrights, painters, and sculptors came to this metropolis to sell their wares and to remain productive. Publishers and other purveyors of letters and the arts were aware of any product that had the promise of benefiting all parties concerned. All in all, the intellectual climate was congenial to the development of a black literature as well as other forms of cultural expression.

Other media through which black talent expressed itself were music and the stage. Plays with Negro themes written and produced by whites provided blacks with opportunities to perform in the legitimate theater, while in the field of lighter entertainment, black performances reached a new high. In serious music, blacks wrote and edited musical scores.

Gradually the scope of this Renaissance made a significant impact on the nation and, in the process, black people became more articulate. There are students who regard this movement as having ended around 1930. Out of the Great Depression years, however, came solid evidence that the creative movement had not ended. The author of the textbook feels that this movement has been an ongoing phenomenon. Black writers continue to be acclaimed for their literary contributions. Opportunities increasingly have widened for the serious black actor. Talented and versatile blacks have had careers that carried them from the New York stage to Hollywood and television, and to significant overseas engagements. There has also been an increase in the number of widely acclaimed black singers, with the color line obtruding only occasionally on the American concert stage.

STUDY NOTES

Pages 361–364, *A new black literature.* In the post-World War I period a distinctive literary movement emerged that directed attention to America's shortcomings. Part of this larger movement, and yet distinct from it, was a kind of literary rebirth among blacks often referred to as the "Harlem Renaissance." America's failure to fulfill its promise of freedom and justice to all left black people defiant, bitter, and impatient. A keener sensitivity to the injustice rampant in the United States, combined with an improved capacity for expression, produced a group of black writers who were in the vanguard of this movement. Even though they produced a literature that for the most part was the expression of a race-conscious group, the propaganda of the communists and socialists got little attention from these writers. They were in revolt not so much against the system as against the way it operated. Notice that not all of the black writers were crusaders for a better world. The element of race in their writings was a natural reflection of their individual and collective experiences. Some wrote with detachment and objectivity while at the same time producing works that were often racial in theme.

Page 364, *Harlem.* New York City was the natural place for the development of the Black Renaissance, since it had been the center of black

America's intellectual and cultural life for a long time. Migrants from the South and other places, such as the British West Indies, made New York's Harlem a colorful and cosmopolitan urban community. Talented people gravitated to Harlem, where they were apt to find a congenial atmosphere in which they could grow professionally and find an outlet for their creative efforts.

Pages 364–371, *The "New York Wits."* Claude McKay is regarded as the "first significant writer of the Harlem Renaissance." Jean Toomer contributed *Cane,* regarded by critics as the single best literary work of the Renaissance. The protests of Countee Cullen "were couched in some of the most delicate, gentle lyrics" of the period. The most cosmopolitan and prolific of the Renaissance writers was Langston Hughes. An experimenter in free verse, he was a true rebel poet, writing often with an air of informality and reflecting the spirit of the "New Negro." Other writers of varying degree of merit appeared. One of the foremost fiction writers was Jessie Redmond Fauset. Her use of characters from well-to-do black families created a new setting in Negro writing. There also was a considerable amount of nonfiction prose, much of it in the pages of monthly publications. Talented blacks could also express themselves through other media. Black actors were afforded opportunities to perform on the legitimate stage. Top-flight black musical revues, such as *Shuffle Along,* furnished a showcase for talented black singers and dancers. In serious music and in the arts, black musicians and artists demonstrated their ability. "Literary parties" attended by the leaders of the Harlem Renaissance afforded one opportunity for these people to mingle and socialize with each other and with representatives of the larger community.

You may want to read the works, or at least some of the poems and stories, of representative figures of the Harlem Renaissance. This is an excellent way of sampling the mood and getting a revealing glimpse of the talent of the individual referred to by Alain Locke as "The New Negro."

Pages 371–381, *The circle widens.* While New York City was the center of the Black Renaissance, it could not claim a complete monopoly on Negro literary activity in the period following the First World War. Even though some students of the cultural awakening feel it ended in 1930, a continuation of it is apparent even today. From the 1940s on, a considerable number of gifted black writers, musicians, actors, painters, and singers have won critical acclaim. You no doubt are familiar with the names and works of some of them, and can attest to their ability to express themselves. Thus, the Renaissance that burst forth in the twenties is still in progress, and was only interrupted by the Great Depression and World War II.

SELF-TEST

Multiple Choice

1. The Harlem Renaissance produced a talented assemblage of black:
   a. professional basketball players.
   b. New York politicians.

c. business leaders.
d. writers.

2. Which one of the following was described as "the most cosmopolitan and "most prolific writer of the Renaissance"?
   a. Claude McKay.
   b. Jean Toomer.
   c. Langston Hughes.
   d. Countee Cullen.

3. A widely acclaimed singer who, on one occasion sang from the steps of the Lincoln Memorial when the Daughters of the American Revolution denied her the use of Constitution Hall in Washington, was:
   a. Marian Anderson.
   b. Leontyne Price.
   c. Camilla Williams.
   d. Dorothy Manor.

4. In the 1940s the best known of the younger black writers was:
   a. John Oliver Killens.
   b. Richard Wright.
   c. Ralph Ellison.
   d. Chester Himes.

5. Of the following, which was responsible for producing the crop of black writers who constituted the Harlem Renaissance?
   a. The desire to stimulate the use of black English.
   b. An attempt to produce literary works for an all-black audience.
   c. A keener realization of injustice and the improvement of the capacity for expression.
   d. The desire to embrace and to publicize the doctrines of socialists and communists.

Fill in the Blanks

1. _____ Cultural movement among talented black writers, musicians, and artists that emerged in New York City after World War I.

2. _____ and _____ These two publications, one of the Urban League and the other of the NAACP, were among the first to open their pages to black poets.

3. _____ Brilliant black musical revue that opened in New York City in the summer of 1921.

4. _____ Many students of the period contend that the Harlem Renaissance ended with this production which appeared in 1930.

5. _____ Written by Ralph Ellison, it received the National Book Award in 1952.

True or False

_____1. Widespread desire for "normalcy" in the twenties discouraged the use of black themes in literature.

_____2. The literature of the Harlem Renaissance was, for the most part, remarkably free of race consciousness.

_____3. Even before the twenties, New York City had become the center of intellectual and cultural life of black America.

_____4. The scope of the Harlem Renaissance gradually encompassed the entire United States.

_____5. Awareness of the gap between the American promise of freedom and his own experiences made the Negro bitter and defiant.

Essay Questions

1. Explain how each of the following helped to bring on the movement called the Harlem Renaissance.
   a. A postwar trend toward increased social consciousness.
   b. Restlessness of the black people.
   c. Improvement of the capacity for expression.
2. How do you account for the development of the Black Renaissance in Harlem, in New York City?
3. Comment briefly on and give the significance of each of the following:
   a. *The Green Pastures*
   b. *Shuffle Along*
   c. Zora Neal Hurston
   d. Arna Bontemps

Identify and/or Define

Renaissance	obtrude	contingent
compeer	timorous	exotic
precursor	docile	Constitution Hall
purveyor		

chapter XXI

THE NEW DEAL

Chronology

1928	Oscar DePriest, a Republican, elected to United States House of Representatives. First black representative from a northern state
1932	Franklin D. Roosevelt elected President
1934	Arthur L. Mitchell elected to Congress. First black Democrat to sit in that lawmaking body
1946	William H. Hastie, first black federal judge, appointed governor of the Virgin Islands

INTRODUCTORY STATEMENT

I N HIS SPEECH accepting the Democratic party's nomination for the presidency, Franklin D. Roosevelt pledged a "new deal" for the American people. The words "new deal" came to be applied as a label for the "reformist social and economic policies and legislative acts" of his administration. New Deal policies were based on the principle that the promises of democracy were goals that could be attained best through planning and controls. This elicited both praise and criticism, with the black masses generally favoring the program. Black people came to regard the relief and recovery policies of the New Deal as beneficial to them, although some blacks criticized the manner in which the relief phases of the program were administered.

Although given little opportunity to participate in the affairs of government, the black man remained an issue in politics from the Civil War to the end of World War I. In the twenties, blacks felt a new hope for greater political power. One consequence of the migration of large numbers of Afro-Americans to the North had been a political resurgence that placed them in the thick of American politics, and brought to them a realization of their potential political power. Traditionally loyal to the Republican party, a number of black voters were sought out by northern Democrats and won over to that party. By 1928, blacks had learned to vote in considerable numbers for candidates who were not Republicans. Even so, it was not easy for black Americans to desert the party of Lincoln completely in the election of 1932. Nevertheless, Roosevelt received substantial black support in that crucial election. The extent of the shift of black allegiance was demonstrated two years later when Arthur W. Mitchell, a black man who had been a registered Republican in 1930, was elected to Congress on the Democratic ticket to replace the black Republican, Oscar DePriest.

Of importance to black citizens was the New Deal policy of securing the assistance of black "specialists and advisors in various government departments." Although not a Roosevelt innovation, his group of advisors was larger in number than they had been in previous administrations. They held significant appointments, were generally not politicians, and were highly trained and intelligent individuals charged with specific functions. Never before had blacks participated in national government affairs as freely and as frequently as they did in this period. The task of these "Black Cabineteers" was to press for the economic and political equality of Afro-Americans.

The organized labor movement was strengthened by New Deal legislation, and in this period faced up to the responsibility of accepting black members. When the CIO was formed with a nucleus of unions in such industries as automobile and steel, it welcomed black workers on an equal basis except in localities where racial tensions existed. Since most black workers were not skilled craftsmen, it was beneficial to be welcomed by an organization adhering to the principle of organizing all workers of a single industry. The positive stand of the CIO Committee to Abolish Racial Discrimination, and the liberal program of its Political Action Committee gave a new hope and a greater sense of security to black laborers.

STUDY NOTES

Pages 383–385, *Political regeneration.* In the decade after World War I, blacks gained new hope for a greater exercise of political power. A realization of that potential in northern urban centers gave them the incentive to exercise a kind of political potency absent since Reconstruction days. In addition to winning offices on the local level, they became more sophisticated concerning national issues and more active on the national level. By 1928, many black voters had become disenchanted with the Republican party. The attempt of that organization to resurrect a strong "lily-white" party in the South prompted a number of prominent black newspapers in 1928 to support Alfred E. Smith, the Democratic candidate for President. The "lily-white" faction advocated the exclusion of black Republicans from both public office and from membership in the party's conventions, a stand supported by Herbert Hoover. The election of Oscar DePriest to Congress in that year gave black voters reason for being optimistic about the future. For the first time in American history, a black man from a northern state sat in the national House of Representatives.

Pages 386–389, *F. D. R. and black folk.* Prior to 1932, few blacks outside New York state were acquainted with Franklin D. Roosevelt. His nomination by the Democratic party for the presidency did not arouse a great deal of enthusiasm in the minds of many black voters, for various reasons. There were other blacks who were reluctant to break with their Republican past and vote for the Democratic ticket. Nevertheless, FDR gained a measure of support from the black electorate. Roosevelt was not long in office before he attracted a large black following. Note in the text-book the reasons for this change of heart. His wife, Eleanor, who by word and action demonstrated her belief in equal opportunity for all, was of great help to the President in this connection. In subsequent campaigns he could count on the support and votes of large numbers of blacks. By 1940, moreover, urban black voters had reached a fairly high level of political sophistication. The author points out that "labor matters, foreign policies, and innumerable other issues influenced the urban Negro voters just as they did the white voters." Greater political awareness was reflected both in voting behavior and in a noticeable increase in the number of black elected officials at state and local levels.

Pages 390–393, *Roosevelt's Black Cabinet.* Other presidents had uti-lized the services of black advisors, but the group chosen by the Roosevelt administration differed from the others in certain important respects, which are enumerated on these pages in your textbook. The aggressive tem-per of black people, a developing war emergency, and the willingness of prominent New Dealers to grant equal opportunities to Afro-Americans served to create a climate in which these black officials could achieve a measure of success.

Pages 393–396, *Government agencies and relief.* By 1935, one sixth of those on relief were blacks, while at the same time they comprised one tenth of the total United States population. There is no doubt that black people benefited from the efforts of New Deal agencies to relieve suffering. But most of the programs ran counter to local laws and long-standing local customs of discriminating against black citizens. Because of this, there appeared variations between black and white relief grants, salaries paid, numbers of workers employed, and the like. Since these federal programs were implemented on the state or local level, the work of such agencies as the Federal Employment Relief Administration was characterized by racial discrimination. Blacks reacted by vigorously attacking the inequities, even though they were appreciative of the benefits derived from such programs. Discrimination continued to be present in the administration of New Deal programs in the South; still some progress was made toward breaking down the patterns of unequal treatment. This led some southern leaders to view the New Deal with distaste and to fret about the concentration of "too much power in Washington."

Pages 398–401, *Black labor and the unions.* With regard to labor, the Roosevelt administration adopted, among other things, a policy of attempting to relieve unemployment and, in the long run, of strengthening organized labor's position in the American economy. The National Labor Relations Act (Wagner Act) of 1935 largely ended the company union practice and made collective bargaining the normal procedure in labor rela-tions. Three years later Congress passed the Fair Labor Standards Act (Wages and Hours) which covered all labor engaged in interstate com-merce, or in the production of goods for interstate commerce. It estab-lished minimum wages and maximum hours of work. Needless to say, many black workers were affected by these measures. However, either because of their exclusion from organized labor unions or because they were engaged in "excluded occupations," several millions received no direct benefits. The successful movement to organize the mass production industries on an industry-wide basis rather than on a craft basis resulted in increased black membership.

SELF-TEST

Multiple Choice

1. Three of the following are true of Oscar DePriest. Which one is *not* true?
   a. His first elective office was that of Chicago alderman.
   b. He was elected to Congress in 1928.
   c. He was the first black Democrat ever to sit in Congress.
   d. His presence in Washington symbolized the regeneration of the black man in politics.

2. Which one of the following was *not* a member of Roosevelt's Black Cabinet?
   a. Harold L. Ickes.
   b. Mary McCleod Bethune.
   c. Ralph Bunche.
   d. Lawrence A. Oxley.

3. As President, Herbert Hoover lost the confidence of blacks for all of the following reasons *except* that:
   a. he supported the lily-white movement in the South.
   b. he appointed an alleged racist to the Supreme Court.
   c. during his administration there was a decline in the patronage given to black Republicans.
   d. he was a Republican, and blacks had traditionally been loyal to the Democratic party.

4. Roosevelt's black advisors differed from earlier ones in which of the following important respects?
   a. The number was larger than previously utilized.
   b. They served in significant official positions.
   c. They were highly trained persons entrusted with specific functions to perform.
   d. all of the above.

5. Which one of the following is *not* a reason why many southern leaders found the New Deal distasteful?
   a. It concentrated too much power in Washington.
   b. Its relief and recovery programs were administered directly from Washington, with no implementation on the local level.
   c. It relieved the suffering of many of those on whose poverty some politicians had climbed to power.
   d. It undertook to force equality in the administration of its benefits.

6. One reason why Roosevelt succeeded in gaining a large following among blacks was that:
   a. he refused to tolerate discrimination in the administration of New Deal relief programs.

b. he dined with Booker T. Washington in the White House.

c. blacks came to regard New Deal economic programs as especially beneficial to them.

d. he established a Negro bureau designed to deal with all matters affecting black people.

True or False

_____1. By 1928, blacks had learned in considerable numbers to vote for candidates who were not Republicans.

_____2. Oscar DePriest was the first black Democrat ever to sit in the Congress.

_____3. Blacks were pleased when President Hoover refused to support the lily-white Republican movement in the South.

_____4. The Great Depression hit the black wage earner with particular severity.

_____5. From its beginning, the CIO sought to organize workers regardless of race or skill.

Essay Questions

1. Describe the political consequences of the concentration of blacks in northern urban centers after World War I.
2. What was the reaction of many black people outside New York state to the candidacy of Franklin D. Roosevelt for the presidency in 1932? *Why*? What caused a significant change in attitude after his election?
3. In what important respects did Roosevelt's group of black advisors differ from earlier presidential advisors?
4. Select three or four of the members of FDR's Black Cabinet and give the responsibilities (job description) of each. Under what handicaps, peculiar to them, did they labor?
5. Identify and give some idea as to what degree black people benefited from each of the following.
   a. Farm Security Administration
   b. Civilian Conservation Corps
   c. National Youth Administration
   d. Committee for Industrial Organization

Identify and/or Define

alderman
disaffection
imperturbable
reapportionment
longshoreman
bloc
electorate

resurgence
New Deal
fireside chat
lily-white
Colored Merchants
   Association

Jobs-for-Negroes
   Movement
Southern Tenant
   Farmers Union

chapter XXII

TWO WORLDS OF RACE

Chronology

1914   The NAACP began the annual awarding of the Spingarn Medal
1915   The Association for the Study of Negro Life and History founded by Carter G. Woodson
1916   *The Journal of Negro History,* edited by Carter G. Woodson, first published
1926   Beginning of annual observance of Negro History week. Period of observance extended in recent years as Black or Afro-American History observance
1940   *Phylon, A Journal of Race and Culture,* edited by W. E. B. DuBois, first published by Atlanta University
1954   *Brown* v. *Board of Education* decision of the Supreme Court outlaws segregated public schools

INTRODUCTORY STATEMENT

I N THE TWENTIETH century, black people continued to manifest a deep and abiding interest in education. Unfortunately, the disparity between tax money spent for the education of white and black children was still apparent. The doctrine of "separate but equal" as established by the U.S. Supreme Court in *Plessy* v. *Ferguson* gave constitutional sanction for many years to state laws requiring separate educational facilities. That these facilities were far from being equal was evident. The momentous and unanimous decision of the Supreme Court in the *Brown* v. *Board of Education* case in 1954 which outlawed segregation in public education, came as a rude shock to many southern whites and caused them to face an unpleasant reality.

Even before the 1954 decision, blacks had sought and obtained Court support for their entrance into southern institutions of higher and professional education. Another medium of education in which black people manifested an interest was the public library. Often compelled to use separate and inadequate facilities, the black reader faced yet another disadvantage in his cultural strivings.

Out of this "confused pattern of education" for Afro-Americans there did emerge a body of highly trained men and women who may be legitimately regarded as eminent scholars.

The black church continued to exert tremendous strength and influence in the black world. In the church, black people found an avenue of self-expression and of recognition, along with opportunities to assume leadership roles. The black press has been of great help in articulating the concerns of the black world.

STUDY NOTES

Pages 402–404, *Trends in education.* The migration of large numbers of Negroes into urban centers did result in some substantial improvement in educational opportunities. A wider tax base in cities could and sometimes did lower the per capita cost of education to the benefit of black children. But even in urban centers in the South, black people in most cases did not receive an equitable share of school appropriations. By 1900, every southern state had enacted laws that provided for separate schools, with those for black children generally of inferior quality. Black schools remained unequal in terms of curriculum, equipment, caliber of instruction, length of school term, and building facilities. By 1945, as a result of direct legal action, differentials between the salaries of black and white teachers were smaller.

Page 404, *Education in the North.* Although segregation in the public schools might have been forbidden by law, *de facto* residential segregation in many northern cities led to separate schools. In certain states, schools were segregated on principle, without regard to law or residence.

Pages 405–408, *Higher education.* By 1955, there were more than 100 institutions for the higher education of blacks in the United States. Whether privately or publicly supported, they were all or predominantly black. Many achieved standards sufficiently high to earn class "A" accreditation from educational rating agencies. Southern black men and women who desired graduate or professional training, by and large, were forced to leave the South to obtain it. A number of states appropriated money for out-of-state graduate training of black students. However, by 1933 it had become apparent that blacks were willing to resort to court action to compel these southern states to discharge their obligations to their black citizens. As a result of court victories spread over a period of time, states were forced to open their graduate and professional facilities to black applicants.

Pages 408–410, *Nullifying the doctrine of "separate but equal."* By 1954 federal courts had noticeably restricted segregation in higher public education and had expanded the opportunities for professional training in southern institutions. As the Supreme Court moved away from the "separate but equal" concept, the South tardily spent more public funds in an attempt to provide better schools for blacks. But the NAACP had already decided to test the validity of segregated elementary and secondary schools. Five pertinent cases were taken to the Court, all of them taking the name *Brown* v. *Board of Education.* The unanimous decision of the Court was that racial segregation in the public schools was unconstitutional. The initial reaction in the South was one of shock, with states in the Deep South assuming a posture of defiance. Note though, that a number of moderate southerners accepted the decision and resigned themselves to implementing it.

Pages 411–412, *Black scholars and publications.* Despite serious difficulties, there did emerge a body of eminent black scholars and literary figures. Although their works were accepted in a number of white journals, some black scholars also founded journals of their own. One of the best known today is the *Journal of Negro History* published since 1916 by the Association for the Study of Negro Life and History. It remains a major source of research and scholarship on the history of black people and you should become familiar with it, if possible.

Pages 412–417, *A separate world.* That a distinctly separate "Negro world" emerged within the American community should not occasion surprise. Segregation in housing became a fixture in cities. This led to a racial homogeneity fostered by municipal ordinances and even by the federal government. Official residential segregation was often buttressed by extra-legal tactics designed to keep the black population within its own ghetto areas. Whether or not these enclaves were made up of the well-to-do class of blacks or of the mass of black workers, they have helped to establish and perpetuate the limits of the black world. Even though there are similarities in interests and tastes between corresponding social classes within the two races, there is seldom enough contact between the two to obliterate racial identity. Thus, to all intents and purposes, the black world continues to exist apart from the larger community. Barred as he was from full participation in the affairs of the larger community, the black man turned to the black church for self-expression, recognition, and leadership. Also important in mirroring and articulating the concerns of the black world are the publications of the black press. By 1979, the number of black newspapers, magazines, and bulletins issued on a regular basis had grown to more than 350. It is understandable that "it was largely the growth of the free, separate black community that provided the greatest stimulation" for the development of the black professional and business class.

Pages 418–421, *Americanization.* Afro-Americans have had to attempt the difficult task of living in two worlds at the same time. Their persistent efforts to enter more fully into the mainstream of American life have frequently been spurned. Thus, for black people, the prospect of complete "Americanization" has remained remote. Along with the "Black Revolution" of the sixties were numerous expressions of black alienation, with some Afro-Americans publicly disavowing any desire to be "Americanized."

SELF-TEST

Multiple Choice

1. Certain trends in the higher education of blacks became noticeable in the second half of the twentieth century. Which of these was *not* one of them?
   a. A dramatic increase in the enrollment of blacks in predominantly white colleges and universities.

b. A marked increase in the number of black administrators in black colleges.

c. Graduate and professional training of blacks decreased noticeably.

d. The number of black administrators in predominantly white colleges increased.

2. Perhaps the most powerful institution in the Negro's world is:
   a. the church.
   b. the public school.
   c. the self-help fraternal organization.
   d. the black press.

3. The Association for the Study of Negro Life and History was founded by:
   a. William E. B. DuBois.
   b. Carter G. Woodson.
   c. William Monroe Trotter.
   d. Booker T. Washington.

4. *Brown* v. *Board of Education* was concerned with:
   a. equal rights for women.
   b. voting rights for black people.
   c. discrimination in the sale of housing.
   d. racial segregation in public schools.

5. By 1900, every state in the South had enacted laws that provided for:
   a. free tuition grants to blacks enrolled in graduate programs in the region's public universities.
   b. separate black and white public schools.
   c. admission of qualified black students to professional predominantly white schools of the section.
   d. a system of integrated elementary schools.

True or False

_____ 1. In the twentieth century, the interest of blacks in education noticeably declined.

_____ 2. The inability of the South to support a dual system of education was reflected largely in its neglect of black schools.

_____ 3. Northern states were not inclined to provide separate schools for black children because of the cost involved.

_____ 4. Institutions of higher learning for blacks decreased in number between 1854 and 1955.

_____ 5. Blacks obtained court support for their entrance into hitherto all-white southern graduate and professional schools.

_____ 6. The existence of a separate black community constitutes one of the remarkable social anomalies of the times.

_____ 7. Protests of blacks against their status reflected a lack of pride in their race and its history.

Essay Questions

1. a. How do you account for the greater opportunities for education for blacks in cities than in rural areas?
   b. What obstacles hindered blacks in their attempts to obtain an education in the South? Be specific.
2. Argue for or against the proposition that the existence of a separate "Negro world" was a positive good. (Try to avoid personal bias.)
3. Discuss the decision of the Supreme Court *Brown* v. *Board of Education,* giving its background and immediate and long-range results.

Take-home Question

4. The decision in *Brown* v. *Board of Education* was written by Chief Justice Earl Warren. His statements have been denounced as sociological rather than legal in basis. Find a copy of the decision and arrive at your own judgment. You should be able to locate both this document and the decision in *Plessy* v. *Ferguson* in a standard book of readings. After having read both decisions, compare the two and account for the differences between them, keeping in mind the years of their appearance and the climate of opinion in these years.

Identify and/or Define

de facto
remand
enclave
alienation
anomaly
Julius Rosenwald Fund
Missouri ex rel. Gaines v. *Canada, Registrar of the University, et al.*

The Association for the Study of Afro-American Life and History (formerly Association for the Study of Negro Life and History)
The Spingarn Medal

chapter XXIII

FIGHTING FOR THE FOUR FREEDOMS

Chronology

1940   Selective Service Act passed by Congress. Forbade discrimination in drafting and training

1940   Colonel B. O. Davis became first black man to be promoted to rank of brigadier general (October)

1941   President Roosevelt issues Executive Order 8802 forbidding racial discrimination in employment in defense industries or government

1945   United Nations organized at San Francisco. Black observers and official delegates in attendance

---

INTRODUCTORY STATEMENT

IN CONTRAST TO their hopes before the First World War, black Americans had no illusions about the benefits they might derive from World War II. Neither did they identify themselves with any of the Axis Powers. But their disheartening experiences in the United States made black people rather skeptical of any benefits that might accrue to them from involvement in the war effort. During the war, articulate Afro-Americans demanded equality of treatment and, in essence, waged two wars—one at home and one overseas. An example of the war on the home front was the battle against job discrimination in defense industries. Progress was made when, in the face of a threat of a massive march on Washington, President Roosevelt issued Executive Order 8802, which officially affirmed the government's policy of nondiscrimination in employment.

In the shooting war, a large number of black soldiers saw combat duty in all theaters of the conflict. For the first time blacks saw service as marines and pilots. Although the army was still segregated, there was little discrimination in the operation of the Selective Service Act, and black officer candidates were trained in the same schools and classes as whites. Unfortunately, attempts of black soldiers to resist segregation and discrimination led to numerous clashes on and off military posts. Toward black

Americans the War Department had a twofold policy: The proportion received into the army would correspond to the proportion of blacks in the total population, and black and white soldiers were to be organized into separate units. Black Americans regarded this as an invidious form of discrimination, and fought its implementation with vigor.

Approximately half a million blacks saw service overseas. The record supports the conclusion that the morale and performance of black troops were adversely affected by the policy of segregation as well as by racial discrimination. Nevertheless, they served their country well; many units received citations for gallantry, with individuals receiving recognition of all types, including the Distinguished Service Cross. As before, black people gave generous support to the war effort on the home front. Many of them, however, indignant and resentful because of mistreatment at home, also supported the *Pittsburgh Courier*'s "Double-V" campaign for victory at home as well as overseas.

The importance that Afro-Americans placed on the establishment of a peace based on justice without regard to race was reflected in a keen interest exhibited in the organizing of the United Nations.

STUDY NOTES

Pages 422–428, *Arsenal of democracy*. The concern of Afro-Americans with world affairs was stimulated by Italy's invasion of the African nation of Ethiopia. Black people shared in a growing distaste for both Mussolini and Hitler and joined in condemning the latter's conquest of smaller European states. After the outbreak of war in Europe in 1939, the United States tried to maintain a neutral position; this policy became increasingly untenable. In the meantime, military and naval preparedness was pushed forward. In 1940, for the first time in American history, Congress passed a compulsory peacetime conscription act. The War Department decided that the proportion of black inductees would correspond to their proportion in the total population and that the army would retain its segregated pattern. Existing black units officered by whites would receive no black line officers. The appointment of blacks to high military and civilian positions failed to convince Negroes that the nation intended to change its commitment to segregated military services. On the job front, blacks still found it difficult to find employment, even as industrial plants began to convert to weapons production. Job discrimination brought forth vigorous protests and led eventually to a presidential order prohibiting discrimination in employment in defense industries. The creation of the Committee on Fair Employment Practices had a salutary effect on the employment of black workers.

Pages 428–437, *Blacks in the service*. Although racial segregation continued within the armed forces, blacks had greater opportunities in this war than in any previous one. The largest number was in the army, but substantial numbers served in the navy, marine corps, and coast guard. There were also black pilots, with two combat units fighting overseas. When the Women's Auxiliary Corps was created, black women were admitted. Twenty-two black outfits participated in ground operations in the European theater, while others saw service in the Mediterranean. Blacks took an active part in the war in the Pacific. Opportunities to serve in the navy expanded when that branch began to enlist blacks for general service. For the first time, the coast guard began to accept blacks in general capacities, and the marine corps began to admit black volunteers for the first time in its history. Unlike the other services, the merchant marine had traditionally practiced a minimum of segregation and discrimination. A number of Liberty ships were named for blacks, and four such ships were commanded by Negro captains.

Pages 437–444, *The home fires.* By the end of the war, few major industries were without at least some black workers, and Negroes were active in bond drives and civilian defense. There was a large migration of blacks out of the South during this war, with a considerable number going to the industrial communities of the Pacific coast. The influx of black people into northern communities raised anew the disturbing specter of racial clashes. Racial tension found dramatic expression in a number of race riots, the most serious of which occurred in Detroit. Other cities averted riots by paying intelligent and careful attention to the problems that spawned such outbreaks. Note that blacks themselves were determined to do all within their power to improve their status. For Afro-Americans, the task of keeping the home fires burning involved the elimination of discrimination and mistreatment. At the end of the war most blacks realized that the struggle to save America's own ideals from destruction had just begun.

Pages 445–449, *The United Nations and human welfare.* Afro-Americans reasoned that through the new United Nations world opinion could be brought to bear on their plight. Of the blacks who attended the organizational meetings in San Francisco, Ralph Bunche was destined to have the greatest impact on the permanent organization. Black leaders saw the UN charter as an important step in focusing world attention on the problems of domestic minorities, including Afro-Americans. The feeling that blacks could use the United Nations to air their domestic grievances led to the filing of a petition with the UN's Economic and Social Council in 1946, by the National Negro Congress. Read the subject matter of this petition, as sketched in the text, and judge for yourself if this action was realistic.

SELF-TEST

Multiple Choice

1. During World War II, four black captains commanded:
   a. destroyers.
   b. Liberty ships.
   c. submarines.
   d. aircraft carriers.

2. By 1940, only four black regular army units were up to full strength. Two of the four were the:
   a. Twenty-second and Twenty-third Infantries.
   b. Seventh and Eighth Cavalries.

    c. Twenty-fourth and Twenty-fifth Infantries.

    d. 369th and 370th Infantries.

3. During World War II, blacks for the first time were permitted to serve in the:

    a. Marine Corps.

    b. infantry.

    c. signal corps.

    d. field artillery.

4. The most serious riot of the period occurred in:

    a. Los Angeles.

    b. Atlanta.

    c. Detroit.

    d. New York.

5. Director of the UN's Trusteeship Council, he was winner of the Nobel Peace Prize in 1950:

    a. W. E. B. DuBois.

    b. E. Franklin Frazier.

    c. Walter White.

    d. Ralph Bunche.

Fill in the Blanks

1. _____ Term applied to the campaign waged by the *Pittsburgh Courier* for victory both at home and overseas.

2. _____ His threat to organize a massive protest march on Washington forced President Roosevelt to issue an executive order forbidding racial discrimination in employment in defense industries.

3. _____ Identify the famous executive order referred to in number 2 above.

4. _____ The first black man to attain the rank of brigadier general in America's armed forces.

5. _____ Organized in San Francisco in 1945, this international body is committed to the settlement of world problems and the maintenance of peace among nations.

True or False

_____1. Because it did not directly affect them, Afro-Americans failed to condemn the fascist movement in Europe.

_____2. Widespread job discrimination in defense industry was completely eliminated by the Committee on Fair Employment Practices.

_____3. Under the Selective Service Act of 1940, more than three million black men registered for service in the armed forces.

_____4. Black and white soldiers were trained in separate officer candidate schools.

_____5. The "Double-V" campaign stood for victory over the Germans as well as over the Japanese.

Essay Questions

1. Compare and contrast the experiences of blacks in World War I and World War II in regard to:
   a. operation of the draft acts
   b. basic training
   c. opportunities to serve in various branches
   d. commissioning of officers
2. Compare and contrast the experiences of black people on the home front in the two wars.
3. a. What aspects of the UN Charter did blacks find pleasing?
   b. Would you say that Afro-Americans were justified in hoping that the United Nations could influence the internal racial policies of the United States? Explain and support your position.
4. Identify, giving the historical significance of each:
   a. Executive Order 8802
   b. B. O. Davis
   c. Dorie Miller
   d. Ted Poston
   e. Ralph Bunche

Identify and/or Define

invidious
accrue
exonerate
cite
intricacy
Axis Powers

Committee on
   Fair Employment
   Practices
United Service
   Organization

"Double-V"
   campaign
United Nations
   Charter

chapter XXIV

THE POSTWAR YEARS

Chronology

1946   Presidential report, *To Secure These Rights,* issued. Concerned with strengthening civil rights for all

1948   Presidential report, *Freedom to Serve,* appeared. Blueprint for integration of armed services

1948   Supreme Court decision in *Shelley* v. *Kraemer* outlaws enforcement of restrictive housing covenants (May)

1955   Interstate Commerce Commission bans racial segregation on interstate carriers as of January 10, 1956

1957   Civil Rights Act enacted by Congress, first since 1875. Marks beginning of new Congressional posture of active participation in area of civil rights legislation

INTRODUCTORY STATEMENT

A FTER WORLD WAR II, the drive to achieve true equality for Afro-Americans was intensified as they pressed harder and more aggressively against the forces of prejudice and discrimination. The injustices that handicapped the black man and woman were more open and flagrant in the South, but they were also apparent in other sections of the United States. Some white Americans, impelled by their consciences and dedicated to freedom and equality, joined black people in the struggle for equal rights.

The role of the federal government in the protection of civil rights changed significantly in the postwar period. It moved from relative non-interference to active participation. The federal courts led the way with decisions that did much to reverse the doctrine of "separate but equal" that had been the long-time pattern in race relations. Following the lead of President Harry S. Truman, the executive departments also joined the struggle by attacking segregation in the armed forces and discrimination in federal employment, and by implementing court decisions and civil rights legislation.

Congress was the last branch of the federal government to act in the area of civil rights. Beginning in 1957, it began to enact civil rights legislation. Although it did not cure all problems, this legislation at least committed the nation to work toward solutions of racial inequities.

As the text points out, this improvement of the status of blacks was "neither uniform nor without vigorous opposition in some quarters." All sorts of obstacles were placed in the path of black advancement, particularly in the South, and often with the open support of the political power structure. Official reaction to the Montgomery bus boycott is illustrative of this. Private groups, such as the White Citizens' Councils, advocating economic reprisals as weapons, joined in the fight to retard the move to desegregate pubic schools. Bearing the brunt of this attack was the NAACP.

STUDY NOTES

Pages 450–455, *Progress.* In several ways, President Harry S. Truman contributed to the creation of a climate in which the status of Afro-Americans could be improved. He accomplished this in part by the issuance of executive orders establishing commissions, two of whose reports are considered in these pages. The continued influx of blacks into the North complicated existing problems in housing and employment, but resulted in gains in political affairs. Activities of such religious groups as the National Council of Churches and the Anti-Defamation League of B'nai B'rith helped foster racial equality. Dining cars and railroad coaches, buses, terminals, and, in the nation's capital, such facilities as hotels were desegregated. There was also a growing tendency to appoint blacks to high posts in the national government.

Pages 455–459, *Reaction.* Vigorous opposition arose in some quarters to the improvement in the status of black people. At times this opposition was clothed in legality, as for example, in the case of the white reaction to the Montgomery bus boycott. At other times new coalitions emerged, utilizing such methods as economic reprisal. The most prominent and most effective of these were the White Citizens' Councils. The battle against school desegregation in the South was fought on a number of fronts, among them being the turning over of public schools to private organizations and the adoption of "freedom of choice" plans. Southern congressmen expressed their resentment of black equality in a "Declaration of Constitutional Principles." In some southern states the NAACP came under attack as a "subversive" organization and was banned. This resistance to change often degenerated into violence, with Negro homes being bombed and, on occasion, black leaders murdered.

Pages 459–462, *The road to revolution.* Widespread resistance to the extension of civil and other rights led blacks to resort to direct and more militant action. Mistreatment by intransigent officials and private citizens, coupled with complacency and indifference elsewhere, ushered in a period of bolder and more aggressive action on the part of Afro-Americans. The Montgomery bus boycott and its success captured the imagination of blacks in other localities and encouraged most of them to operate within the system to seek improvement. Giving encouragement was the positive stand taken by the federal government. Beginning with the passage of the

Civil Rights Act of 1957, Congress began to participate more actively in the effort to secure civil rights for black Americans. Become familiar with the provisions of this act. For one thing, it elevated the Civil Rights Section of the Justice Department to the status of a division. For another, it created the United States Commission on Civil Rights. The new law's primary feature empowered the Attorney General to seek court injunctions against the obstruction or deprivation of voting rights. You will notice that it required court proceedings, which were often protracted, a condition that was not remedied until the passage of the Voting Rights Act of 1965.

SELF-TEST

Multiple Choice

1. All of the following were true of the report, *To Secure These Rights,* except that it:
   a. denounced the denial of civil rights to some.
   b. called for a positive program to strengthen civil rights.
   c. was specifically intended to be a blueprint for integration of the armed forces.
   d. urged the elimination of racial segregation from American life.

2. Which of the following was the last branch of the federal government to move actively in the area of civil rights for Negroes?
   a. the executive.
   b. the legislative.
   c. the judicial.

3. Economic actions invoked against blacks who were active in civil rights in the 1950s included:
   a. dismissals from jobs.
   b. denials of loans.
   c. foreclosures of mortgages.
   d. all of the above.

4. Southern leaders fought school desegregation in several ways. Which of these was *not* one of them?
   a. turning schools over to private organizations.
   b. encouraging "voluntary segregation."
   c. threatening to secede from the Union.
   d. adopting "freedom of choice" plans.

5. When the American Federation of Labor merged with the CIO, these two black men were elected vice-presidents of the new organization:
   a. A. Philip Randolph and Willard Townsend.
   b. William Hastie and Thurgood Marshall.
   c. Scovel Richardson and Hulan Jack.
   d. William Dawson and Adam Clayton Powell.

True or False

_____1. President Truman contributed to the creation of a climate in which the status of blacks was officially degraded.

_____2. The report, *To Secure These Rights,* strongly denounced the efforts of Afro-Americans to secure civil rights.

_____3. A battlefield test of armed forces integration received its first widespread application in Korea.

_____4. The political influence of blacks increased substantially in the post-World War II decades.

_____5. Southern resistance to any change in the status of black people often degenerated into violence.

Essay Questions

1. In what significant ways did President Truman throw the weight of his office behind the drive for equal rights for Afro-Americans? Be specific.
2. Comment on the role of the following in improving the position of black people in American life.
   a. religious bodies
   b. labor unions
   c. the Interstate Commerce Commission
3. Write a short essay on the reaction of white southerners to the improvement in the status of blacks in the fifties. Illustrate your discussion with examples.
4. Give the basic provisions of and significance of the Civil Rights Act of 1957. What was a chief weakness of the act?
5. Identify and give the historical significance of:
   a. General Matthew Ridgway
   b. Judge J. Waties Waring
   c. Judge Thurgood Marshall
   d. Autherine Lucy

Identify and/or Define

civil rights
restrictive covenant
intransigence
sanctions
injunction
subversive

protract
interposition
nullification
reprisal
Dixiecrat party
"Southern Manifesto"

Black Monday
"Uptown Ku Klux Klans"
U.S. Commission on Civil Rights

chapter XXV

THE BLACK REVOLUTION

Chronology

1960   The sit-in movement began by four North Carolina Agricultural and Technical College students in Greensboro, North Carolina (February)
1960   Civil Rights Act signed by President Eisenhower
1961   Congress of Racial Equality-sponsored Freedom Riders challenged segregation on interstate carriers in South
1963   Massive protest—March on Washington
1964   Civil Rights Act. Forbade discrimination in public accommodations and federally assisted programs
1964   Martin Luther King, Jr., awarded Nobel Peace Prize
1965   Voting Rights Act. Widened opportunities for blacks to register to vote
1966   Robert C. Weaver became Secretary of Housing and Urban Development; first black Cabinet member
1967   Thurgood Marshall appointed to the U.S. Supreme Court; first black member of that tribunal

INTRODUCTORY STATEMENT

BY THE TIME four students from North Carolina Agricultural and Technical challenged the segregated food service arrangements in a Greensboro variety store in February 1960, "the stage was already set for the beginning" of the Black Revolution. The changes in the status of Afro-Americans themselves, along with such other facets of the Revolution as the changes in the way that black people viewed themselves, represent the subject matter of this chapter.

In the decade of the sixties, the national government continued its active role in the civil rights arena. Civil rights legislation was welcomed by blacks who were disposed to operate within the political system, but it became clear that these laws did not cure basic problems. It was equally as clear that intransigent whites had little, if any, intention of adhering to the provisions of these laws. Frustrated and impatient urban blacks, bitter because they felt that nonviolence had led to little improvement in their lot, turned to alternative—and sometimes violent—solutions. Race riots, often confined to ghettos, along with an intensification of resistance on the part of some whites to any improvements in the status of black Americans, were dramatic indications of a troubled and divided society.

Long active in the struggle for equality, the NAACP and the Urban League were joined by such newer groups as the Congress of Racial Equality, the Southern Christian Leadership Conference (founded in 1957 by Dr. Martin Luther King, Jr.), and the Student Nonviolent Coordinating Committee. Dr. King became the chief spokesman and exponent of nonviolent methods of achieving equality. "Black Power" became the goal in the midsixties of alienated militants disillusioned with the slow rate of social change. To some, the slogan suggested black aggressiveness within the framework of existing society; to others it meant withdrawal from the mainstream of American society with a repudiation of nonviolent action.

Even though some Afro-Americans concluded that they could expect only meager gains operating within the framework of the established system, most opted to remain within the folds of the two-party system. Few argued that the political process in the midseventies represented a panacea, but there is a strong feeling that black elected officials are in a position to see that the black community will receive more benefits. At this point, Afro-Americans can correctly visualize themselves as having been active in the ongoing struggle for freedom.

Afro-Americans traditionally have viewed their destiny as inextricably connected with the fate of darker peoples throughout the world, and especially with those in "Mother Africa." Realizing that they have become an integral part of Western culture and civilization, they still recognize and take pride in their African heritage.

STUDY NOTES

Pages 463–465, *The beginnings.* The sit-in movement began in 1960. It spread and assumed massive proportions, with many participants arrested for trespassing, disorderly conduct, and disobeying police officers. It subsequently received assistance from such groups as the existing Congress of Racial Equality but it was mainly student-centered and led. To coordinate the movement the Student Nonviolent Coordinating Committee was founded. By the time the students launched the sit-in technique, the stage was set for the beginnings of the Black Revolution. The road to revolution had been paved by Supreme Court decisions, the Montgomery bus boycott, and the emergence of Dr. Martin Luther King, Jr. In 1960, Congress passed another civil rights bill. Read its basic provisions, noting how it differed from or complemented the 1957 act and the one that followed in 1964.

Pages 465–468, *The Kennedy years.* In 1960, large numbers of blacks gave their votes to John F. Kennedy for President. He lent "moral" support to the continuing struggle for equality and appointed blacks to important federal positions. In the spring of 1961, CORE tested and protested segregation in interstate transportation by sending "freedom riders" into the South. These and other such travelers, when not escorted by federal marshals, were often attacked by angry whites. School desegregation in the South moved with exasperating slowness, while *de facto* segregation in the North remained firmly entrenched.

Pages 468–471, *Demonstrations and the March on Washington.* By 1963, blacks had discovered the potency of demonstrations and so the practice increased. Many demonstrations supported better job opportunities and an end to *de facto* segregation in education and housing in the North. Legislation was sent to Congress to rectify inequities, but bitter opposition was shown to these proposals. As Congress debated a proposed bill, a large assemblage of blacks and whites staged the massive "March on Washington for Jobs and Freedom," the largest demonstration the capital had ever experienced. The assassination of President Kennedy brought Lyndon B. Johnson to the presidency.

Pages 472–475, *Johnson and the Civil Rights Act of 1964.* When Johnson became President, he promptly made known his full support for the late President Kennedy's civil rights program. A far-reaching and comprehensive law was finally enacted. Read the basic provisions of this legislation, and become familiar with its chief features. There was a noticeable decline in discrimination in some fields following this act. However, a "white backlash" emerged as it went into effect.

Pages 475–480, *The Voting Rights Act of 1965.* Despite existing civil rights legislation, thousands of Negroes in the South were denied the right to register and vote. Demonstrators who attempted to dramatize the plight of the black would-be voter were the victims of acts of violence. One of the more widely observed events was the Selma-to-Montgomery march of thousands of people from all over the country who gathered in support of the demonstrators. This was part of the background for the new Voting Rights Act of 1965. Notice that its provisions applied to states and counties primarily in the South. Greater opportunity to participate in the political process as an equal was of value to black citizens, but it became clear that this did not solve the problems of discrimination in such areas as housing and job opportunities. The economic gap between blacks and whites did not narrow to an appreciable degree in the 1960s. The appointment of "token" blacks to highly visible, prestigious positions in government and in the private sector failed to lessen the disparity between the races. Racial tension in the nation was dramatized by the disturbances in the Watts area of Los Angeles in the summer of 1965. The underlying cause of this racial disturbance was the "demoralization" of the city's black population.

Pages 481–484, *Illusion of equality.* Much has been said and written about black "militants" and a sense of race pride as expressed in slogans, dress, and demands of some Afro-Americans. Note comments made in the text and you will perhaps understand more clearly the extent of the disillusionment, bitterness, and defiance of these Negro Americans. Notice the reference to Stokely Carmichael and his coining of the phrase "Black Power." Adding to the impatience of black Americans was the slow pace of school desegregation in both the South and the North, where *de facto* segregation was often the rule. Certain provisions of the 1964 Civil Rights Act helped prod school boards into action. Because of long-established housing patterns in many cities, it became necessary to rely on busing as a means of desegregating schools or of achieving racial balance. This was a solution bitterly assailed and opposed by many.

Pages 484–487, *Revolution at high tide.* The "Black Revolution" of the 1960s was characterized by such direct-action tactics as sit-ins, freedom rides, marches, and demonstrations. Of prime importance to its goals were voter registration drives. Intense opposition from conservative whites had the effect of building up a feeling of cynicism among many black Americans, some of whom concluded that under no circumstances would justice and equality be extended to them. The assassination of Martin L. King, Jr., was the final blow. It affirmed the feeling among militant, action-oriented blacks that whites would only respond negatively to peaceful, nonviolent demands for equality. Out of this feeling arose a more militant aspect of the revolution as reflected in the programs of such new organizations as the Black Panther Party for Self-Defense. Another reflection of deep suspicion of America's "good intentions" is found in the "Black Manifesto" issued by the Black Economic Development Conference in 1969. A more permanent aspect of the Revolution was the noticeable increase in the political power of Afro-Americans, a power that has not yet reached its fullest potential.

Pages 492–503, *Balance sheet of the Revolution.* Progress has been made, particularly in the political arena. Continued progress will depend on the extent to which black people register and actually go to the polls. In the last quarter of this century a Negro middle class is continuing to grow in size and influence. More financial rewards are accruing from such disparate sources as business enterprises and the entertainment field. From the vantage point of the midseventies, Afro-Americans can visualize themselves as active participants with other like-minded groups in the ongoing struggle for freedom in the United States. They were, in a real sense, the nation's conscience and a constant reminder of its shortcomings. They "had become an integral part of Western culture and civilization, and their fate was inextricably connected with it."

SELF-TEST

Written Assignment: Matching

Number an answer sheet from 1 to 7. Beside each number, put the *letter* of the matching term.

　　　　a. The Civil Rights Act of 1960
　　　　b. The Civil Rights Act of 1964
　　　　c. The Voting Rights Act of 1965

_b_ 1.　Required the elimination of discrimination in federally assisted projects and programs (Title VI).

_a_ 2.　Required that voting records be preserved for twenty-two months following any primary, special, or general election.

_c_ 3.　Suspended all literacy tests and similar voting qualifications in states and counties where less than 50 percent of the adults had voted in the previous year.

_a_ 4.　Singled out for punishment anyone found guilty of defacing churches, synagogues, or other buildings.

_b_ 5. Established a federal Equal Employment Opportunity Commission.

_a_ 6. Provided for direct federal action to enable Negroes to register and vote.

_b_ 7. Guaranteed access to public accommodations such as hotels.

Fill in the Blanks

1. _Twenty-Fourth amendment_ This amendment outlawed the requirement of the poll tax, long a means of disfranchising Negroes in federal elections.

2. _Thurgood Marshall_ Appointed an Associate Justice of the U.S. Supreme Court, he is the first and only black man to occupy a seat on that bench.

3. _Black Power_ This widely quoted expression was an articulation of the impatience and disillusionment of civil rights militants with the slow rate of social change in the midsixties.

4. _de Facto_ This kind of segregation, often found in the North, results from the concentration of blacks in certain well-defined geographic areas, rather than from statutory regulation.

5. _Sit-in_ This youth-oriented tactic, aimed at desegregating facilities, began in Greensboro, North Carolina, in 1960.

True or False

_T_ 1. Both his religion and his age made Kennedy unique among United States Presidents.

_F_ 2. Kennedy's religion made him unacceptable to the vast majority of black voters.

_F_ 3. President Johnson was much less successful than Kennedy in securing enactment of civil rights legislation.

_T_ 4. The term _nonviolence_ is closely associated with the early years of the Black Revolution.

_T_ 5. Blacks discovered that demonstrations often accomplished what other tactics had not.

_F_ 6. Increased black voter registration ended the struggle for equality.

_F_ 7. A combination of executive action and federal legislation was successful in preventing the outbreak of racial violence in the midsixties.

Essay Questions

1. Argue for or against the proposition that the "Black Revolution" of the 1960s was successful in achieving all its goals, both immediate and long-range.
2. Comment on any five of the following:
   a. The Montgomery bus boycott
   b. March on Washington for Jobs and Freedom
   c. The Watts riot
   d. The freedom riders
   e. Black Power
   f. Student Nonviolent Coordinating Committee
   g. Black Panther Party for Self-Defense
   h. National Black Political Convention of 1972

Identify and/or Define

"massive tokenism" Patricia Harris "Black Manifesto"
pejorative Andrew Young freedom riders
ambivalence Wade McCree PUSH
caucus CORE Congressional Black
recalcitrant SNCC Caucus
disparate SCLC Voter Education
practitioner "Black Power" Project

KEY TO SELF-TEST

chapter I

Multiple Choice	*Fill in the Blanks*	*True or False*
1. (b)	1. Mecca	1. F
2. (d)	2. Mali	2. F
3. (a)	3. Sundiata Keita	3. T
4. (c)	4. Askia Mohammed	4. T
5. (b)	5. Slave trade	5. T

chapter II

Multiple Choice	*Fill in the Blanks*	*True or False*
1. (a)	1. The kingdom	1. F
2. (d)	2. Electing family	2. T
3. (c)	3. Ancestor worship	3. F
4. (a)	4. The family	4. T
5. (c)	5. The song	5. F

chapter III

Multiple Choice	*Fill in the Blanks*	*True or False*
1. (d)	1. Renaissance and	1. F
2. (a)	Commercial	2. T
3. (c)	Revolution	3. F

chapter III
(continued)

Multiple Choice	*Fill in the Blanks*	*True or False*
4. (b)	2. Fourteenth	4. T
5. (c)	3. Estevanico	5. F
	4. Indentured servant (voluntary)	
	5. Portugal	

chapter IV

Multiple Choice	*Fill in the Blanks*	*True or False*
1. (c)	1. tobacco	1. F
2. (b)	2. Spain	2. T
3. (c)	3. seasoning	3. F
4. (d)	4. slave or black codes	4. F
5. (c)	5. Maroons	5. T

chapter V

Multiple Choice	*Fill in the Blanks*	*True or False*
1. (d)	1. Virginia	1. F
2. (c)	2. Georgia	2. F
3. (a)	3. Quakers	3. T
4. (b)	4. New England	4. T
5. (d)	5. New York	5. T
6. (d)		
7. (c)		
8. (b)		

chapter VI

Multiple Choice	*Fill in the Blanks*	*True or False*
1. (d)	1. Viceroyalty of New Granada	1. T
2. (c)	2. Brazil	2. F
3. (a)	3. *Asiento*	3. F
4. (b)	4. Republic of Palmares	4. F
	5. Haiti	5. T

chapter VII

Multiple Choice	Fill in the Blanks	True or False
1. (c)	1. 1763	1. F
2. (d)	2. Georgia and South Carolina	2. F
3. (a)	3. Boston Massacre	3. T
4. (d)	4. Lord John Murray Dunmore	4. T
5. (a)	5. Abigail Adams	5. T

chapter VIII

Multiple Choice	Fill in the Blanks	True or False
1. (b)	1. Boston	1. T
2. (c)	2. Eli Whitney	2. T
3. (d)	3. Toussaint L'Ouverture	3. F
4. (a)	4. Free African Society	4. F
5. (c)	5. Richard Allen	5. F

chapter IX

Multiple Choice	Fill in the Blanks	True or False
1. (b)	1. The frontier	1. F
2. (a)	2. James P. Beckwourth	2. T
3. (d)	3. war hawks	3. F
4. (c)	4. War of 1812	4. T
5. (d)	5. Northwest Ordinance	5. T

chapter X

Multiple Choice	Fill in the Blanks	True or False
1. (b)	1. Planters	1. F
2. (c)	2. Slave codes	2. F

chapter X
(continued)

Multiple Choice	*Fill in the Blanks*	*True or False*
3. (d)	3. Summer lay-by	3. F
4. (a)	and Christmas	4. T
5. (d)	4. Patrol	5. T
	5. Gang	6. F
		7. T
		8. F
		9. T
		10. T

chapter XI

Multiple Choice	*Fill in the Blanks*	*True or False*
1. (c)	1. Free	1. F
2. (b)	2. North Star	2. T
3. (d)	3. *Christian Herald*	3. T
4. (d)	4. American	4. F
5. (a)	Colonization	5. F
	Society	6. T
	5. Certificate of	7. F
	freedom	8. F
		9. T
		10. T

chapter XII

Multiple Choice	*Fill in the Blanks*	*True or False*
1. (b)	1. William L.	1. F
2. (c)	Garrison	2. T
3. (d)	2. American Anti-	3. T
4. (b)	Slavery Society	4. F
5. (a)	3. Liberty party	5. F
	4. "gag rule"	
	5. Underground	
	Railroad	

chapter XIII

Multiple Choice

1. (c)
2. (d)
3. (c)
4. (b)
5. (d)

Fill in the Blanks

1. Maryland
2. Confiscation Act
3. American Missionary Association
4. David Hunter
5. 54th Massachusetts Regiment

True or False

1. T
2. T
3. F
4. T
5. F

chapter XIV

Multiple Choice

1. (a)
2. (b)
3. (b)
4. (c)
5. (d)
6. (a)
7. (c)
8. (d)

Fill in the Blanks

1. Thirteenth Amendment
2. Black Codes
3. Freedmen's Bureau
4. Francis L. Cardozo
5. Fourteenth

True or False

1. F
2. T
3. F
4. T
5. T
6. F
7. T
8. F
9. F
10. T

chapter XV

Multiple Choice

1. (d)
2. (a)
3. (b)
4. (d)
5. (b)

Fill in the Blanks

1. Union League
2. Georgia
3. South Carolina, Florida, Louisiana
4. *United States* v. *Cruikshank*
5. Populist party

True or False

1. F
2. T
3. T
4. T
5. F

chapter XVI

Multiple Choice	*Fill in the Blanks*	*True or False*
1. (b)	1. B. T. Washington	1. T
2. (d)	2. Frederick Douglass	2. F
3. (c)	3. Knights of Labor	3. F
4. (d)	4. George Washington	4. T
5. (c)	Williams	5. F
	5. W. E. B. DuBois	

chapter XVII

Multiple Choice	*Fill in the Blanks*	*True or False*
1. (b)	1. The *Maine*	1. F
2. (b)	2. Charles Young	2. T
3. (c)	3. Muckrakers	3. T
4. (d)	4. W. E. B. DuBois	4. F
5. (d)	5. National Urban	5. F
	League	

chapter XVIII

Multiple Choice	*Fill in the Blanks*	*True or False*
1. (c)	1. Ninety-Second	1. T
2. (d)	2. 369th U.S. Infantry	2. F
3. (c)	3. Emmett J. Scott	3. F
4. (b)	4. The *Messenger*	4. T
5. (d)	5. "Battle of Henry	5. T
	Johnson"	

chapter XIX

Multiple Choice	*Fill in the Blanks*	*True or False*
1. (b)	1. "Red Summer"	1. F
2. (c)	2. Marcus Garvey	2. F

chapter XIX
(continued)

Multiple Choice	*Fill in the Blanks*	*True or False*
3. (a)	3. Universal Negro	3. T
4. (d)	Improvement	4. F
5. (c)	Association	5. T
	4. Brotherhood of	
	Sleeping Car	
	Porters and	
	Maids	
	5. Ku Klux Klan	

chapter XX

Multiple Choice	*Fill in the Blanks*	*True or False*
1. (d)	1. Harlem Renaissance	1. F
2. (c)	2. *Opportunity* and	2. F
3. (a)	*Crisis*	3. T
4. (b)	3. *Shuffle Along*	4. T
5. (c)	4. *The Green Pastures*	5. T
	5. *The Invisible Man*	

chapter XXI

Multiple Choice	*Fill in the Blanks*	*True or False*
1. (c)	NONE	1. T
2. (a)		2. F
3. (d)		3. F
4. (d)		4. T
5. (b)		5. T
6. (c)		

chapter XXII

Multiple Choice	*Fill in the Blanks*	*True or False*
1. (c)	NONE	1. F

chapter XXII

(continued)

Multiple Choice	*Fill in the Blanks*	*True or False*
2. (a)		2. T
3. (b)		3. F
4. (d)		4. F
5. (b)		5. T
		6. T
		7. F

chapter XXIII

Multiple Choice	*Fill in the Blanks*	*True or False*
1. (b)	1. "Double-V"	1. F
2. (c)	2. A. Philip Randolph	2. F
3. (a)	3. Executive Order	3. T
4. (c)	8802	4. F
5. (d)	4. B. O. Davis	5. F
	5. United Nations	

chapter XXIV

Multiple Choice	*Fill in the Blanks*	*True or False*
1. (c)	NONE	1. F
2. (b)		2. F
3. (d)		3. T
4. (c)		4. T
5. (a)		5. T

chapter XXV

Multiple Choice	*Fill in the Blanks*	*True or False*
1. (b)	1. Twenty-fourth	1. T
2. (a)	Amendment	2. F
3. (c)	2. Thurgood	3. F
4. (a)	Marshall	4. T
5. (b)	3. "Black Power"	5. T
6. (c)	4. *de facto*	6. F
7. (b)	5. sit-in	7. F

ABOUT THE AUTHOR

E DWARD F. SWEAT is Fuller E. Callaway Professor Emeritus of History at Clark College in Atlanta, Georgia. At present, he is a lecturer in Afro-American history at Allen University in Columbia, South Carolina. He is author of *History of the American Negro: USAFI Study Guide,* the monographs *The Economic Status of Free Blacks in Antebellum Georgia* (1974) and *Free Blacks and the Law in Antebellum Georgia* (1976), and articles that have appeared in *The Journal of Negro History, Phylon,* and the *Atlanta Historical Journal.*